Famous mathematicians

Learning from the lives of key thinkers

Activities for Key Stage 2

John Davis

QUESTIONS PUBLISHING

27 Frederick Street, Birmingham B1 3HH

First published in 2000 by
The Questions Publishing Company Ltd
27 Frederick Street, Birmingham B1 3HH

Designed and typeset by Keystroke, Jacaranda Lodge, Wolverhampton
Edited by Audrey Bamber
Illustrations by Jane Bottomley
Cover design by James Davies

ISBN: 1-84190-028-1

Contents

Introduction   1

1 Eratosthenes: Shaking out the primes   3

2 John Napier: Picking the bones out of multiplication   15

3 Blaise Pascal: Investigating triangles   27

4 Leonardo Fibonacci: Finding patterns all around us   39

5 René Descartes: Thinking your way to a solution   49

6 Archimedes: Putting ideas into action   61

7 Euclid: Writing a Greek bestseller   71

8 Pythagoras: Studying in quietness and solitude   83

9 Leonhard Euler: Working on through blindness   95

10 Gottfried Leibniz: Paving the way for computers   107

   Answers and solutions   119

   Index   125

Introduction

The introduction of the formal daily maths lesson in primary schools has certainly heightened children's awareness of the subject and the importance it plays in their everyday lives. But how much do they know about the background of the mathematics they are being taught and the personalities throughout history who have been instrumental in the inclusion of these topics in the school curriculum?

Children may become familiar with the name Fibonacci during work on number sequences but who was this Italian, when did he live and why is his work still relevant today? Why is a rule about the properties of certain special triangles called Pythagoras' Theorem, how would you use Eratosthenes' sieve and what does Archimedes' Principle have to do with measuring capacity? Why do we find positions using Cartesian co-ordinates and in what way is a piece of seventeenth-century equipment called Napier's Bones linked to the modern electronic calculator? This book will help children to answer these questions and to find out much more.

The book contains chapters on the life and work of ten famous mathematicians whose reputation and influence not only spans the last millennium but continues to effect teaching in 2000 – designated officially as International Maths Year – and beyond.

Each chapter opens with biographical information about the mathematician and puts him into his historical setting. There are details of the contribution each has made, not only to mathematics but also in other fields, particularly science, astronomy and religion, and there is scope to follow these up in other areas of the curriculum. This section has been written for children to read and can be photocopied for use as a piece of factual information during the text level part of the daily Literacy Hour.

The main part of each chapter then describes how their work relates to primary school maths teaching today and includes a range of differentiated practical classroom-based tasks for children to carry out. The purpose of the activities outlined is to supplement, enrich and extend work being done by Key Stage 2 children during the daily maths lesson. The accent is very much on a problem-solving, investigative approach to learning in mathematics and is aimed at enabling children to become more versatile in the way in which they reason, make deductions and apply their mathematical knowledge and skills. Many of these tasks could be followed up as homework, particularly as it would encourage children to think in terms of maths activities away from the usual classroom environment. Much of the information might also appeal to parents.

Suggestions are given at the end of each chapter about how to support lower-ability children and there are ideas about extension work for those in the higher-ability range. Because language is such a crucial aspect of mathematics teaching, a list of essential vocabulary is included and all the practical tasks are cross-referenced to the National Numeracy Strategy Framework with the focus aimed particularly at Years 4 and 6. Details are also given about the resources needed to carry out and follow up tasks and each chapter contains two photocopiable activities to get children started.

1
Eratosthenes
Shaking out the primes

Scientists and mathematicians who set out today to find accurate measurements of the Earth's circumference have a wide range of technical and scientific equipment that they can use.

But over 2000 years ago, around 200 BC, a scholar in the country we now call Egypt was getting very close to the precise answer by using a simple angle measurer, some human pacers, a deep well and the rays of the sun.

The scholar's name was Eratosthenes. We know little about his actual life, apart from the fact that he was in charge of the library at Alexandria, but much of the work he did in both astronomy, geography and mathematics helped later scholars to understand more about the world in which they lived.

Eratosthenes based his calculations about the Earth's circumference on two towns in Egypt, which his official pacers measured were 800 kilometres (500 miles) apart. Pacers were people who used to walk or pace out the distance between locations if accurate measurements were needed. The two towns Eratosthenes chose were Alexandria, where he worked, and a settlement further south which was then known as Syene but today is called Aswan.

He observed that on Midsummer's Day at noon in Aswan the sun was directly overhead. He knew this because he could see its rays shining on the bottom of a deep well. Meanwhile at Alexandria, 800 kilometres to the north, the sun's rays were measured at an angle of 7 degrees at the same time on the same day (see Figure 1.1).

He correctly assumed that since the Earth and the Sun were a very long distance away from each other, the sun's rays were probably parallel when they reached the Earth. Eratosthenes calculated from this that the distance between the two towns, 800 kilometres, was about one-fiftieth of the Earth's circumference (7/360 degrees). 800 × 50 produces an answer of exactly 40,000 kilometres. The actual units he used for his measurements are not known. The problem is that although a unit called a stadia was used in Egypt at that time to measure distances, the length of a stadia could vary from one place to another. Even bearing this in mind, Eratosthenes' calculation is extremely close to modern measurements which puts the Earth's circumference at 40,024 kilometres (24,870 miles).

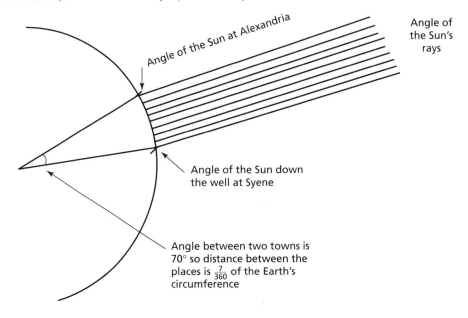

● **Figure 1.1**

This was just one of Eratosthenes' many interests. During his travels in Egypt he was able to sketch a virtually correct route of the River Nile and suggest that the source of the river was in fact a lake. His book *Geographica* was the first to use the word 'geography' as a title.

He also recorded the positions of 675 fixed stars, wrote poems and took a keen interest in the theatre. He spent some time working on a calendar that included leap years and tried to fix the dates of important events he knew about, dating from the time when the Greeks laid siege to the city of Troy.

Use the information to find the answers to questions such as:

- Which numbers are square numbers only?
- Which numbers are multiples of 4 and 6?
- Which numbers are square numbers and multiples of 4?
- Why does 36 appear in all three circles?

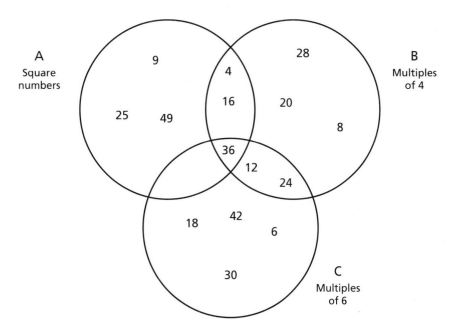

• **Figure 1.4:** Venn diagram

Children should be able to produce their own Venn diagrams using multiples of other numbers and also incorporate members of other special number families like odd and even.

Factor trees

Introduce the children to work on factors and primes with a look at factor trees. These can be drawn by splitting up numbers into multiplication facts. Some examples are shown in Figure 1.5. Through discussion help children to realise that the final roots of any factor tree will always be the same and will always end with what are known as prime factors (Figure 1.6).

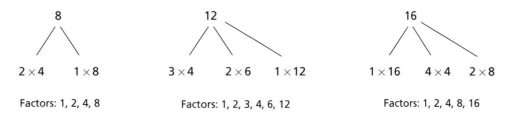

• **Figure 1.5:** Factor trees

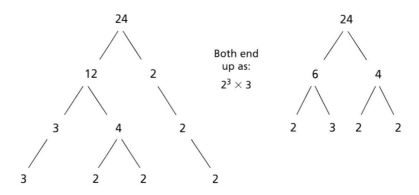

Both end up as:

$2^3 \times 3$

• **Figure 1.6**

Then try this activity. Make a table of the factors of numbers up to 30, or higher if you wish (Figure 1.7). What can be said about the numbers with only two factors? Most of the numbers have an even number of factors. But which numbers have an odd number and what is special about them?

Number	Factors	Number of factors
1	1	1
2	1, 2	2
3	1, 3	2
4	1, 2, 4	3
5	1, 5	2
6	1, 2, 3, 6	4
7	1, 7	2
8	1, 2, 4, 8	4
9	1, 3, 9	3
10	1, 2, 5, 10	4
and so on		

• **Figure 1.7**

Dice game

Children can work in pairs to play a factor game using dice. Each child throws two dice to make a two-digit number. If the numbers 4 and 8 are thrown the number chosen could be either 48 or 84. This should be repeated twice more so that each child has three two-digit numbers. Each child should then write down all the factors for all three of their numbers and when they are added together the bigger total wins. There is one extra rule: 1 and the number itself should not be counted.

USING ERATOSTHENES' SIEVE

Next use the Eratosthenes' sieve method to find all the prime numbers between 1 and 100. This should be done using a 100 square. One has been provided on the photocopiable sheet *Shaking out the primes*. Emphasise that instructions must be followed carefully in order to obtain an accurate result:

- Start from 2 and count in twos, crossing out the numbers with a coloured pencil. Do not cross out 2.
- Start from 3 and count in threes, striking out every third number. Do not cross out 3.
- Start from 5 and count in fives, marking out every fifth number. Do not cross out 5.
- Start from 7 and count in sevens, crossing out every seventh number. Do not cross out 7.
- Use a different coloured pencil to circle all the numbers that remain.

Discuss why some numbers have been crossed more than once. The circled numbers are the prime numbers. If 1 is not included, for the reasons already explained, there should be 25 of them.

Once the prime numbers between 1 and 100 have been found, ask the children to use them to test out certain propositions and theories:

1 Is it true that every even number bigger than 6 can be written as the sum of two prime numbers? It works for 5 + 7 = 12 and 7 + 13 = 20, but are there others?
2 Look carefully at all the prime numbers between 5 and 100. Divide each one by 6. What is significant about the remainders? Is there an explanation why this happens?
3 Find out what happens if numbers are turned into shapes on squared paper. Counters or buttons could be used or draw coloured dots. Is it true to say that any number that cannot be made into a square or a rectangle is a prime number? Try some out (Figure 1.8).

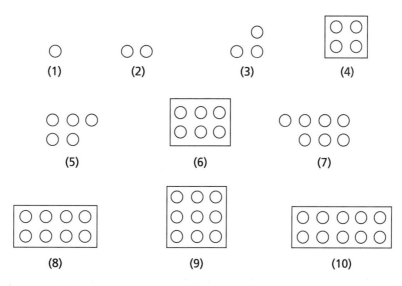

• **Figure 1.8**

4   Say whether these statements are true or false. No even number, except 2, can be a prime number. No prime number more than 5 can end with 5. The digits of a prime number can never add up to 9 or a member of the 9× table. Every even number under 10 can be made from the difference between two consecutive prime numbers.

SYMMETRY

Finally, link knowledge of prime numbers with shape work. These examples of reflective symmetry have been made on squared paper using prime numbers. Working in 5 × 3 grids, challenge the children to create patterns with at least one or possibly two lines of symmetry. Some examples are shown in Figure 1.9 for the prime numbers 5 and 7. Investigate 9, 11 and 13. Check solutions are accurate by using plastic mirrors.

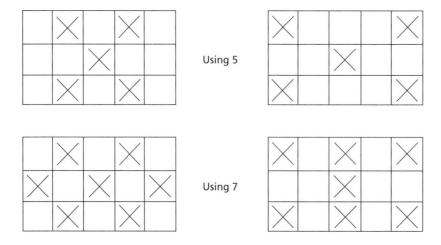

• **Figure 1.9:** Symmetrical patterns with prime numbers

SUPPORT

As work on multiples, factors and primes involves knowledge and understanding of the times tables between 2 and 10, some children will need the help of multiplication or table squares to carry out these activities. Limit the task on factor trees initially to multiples of 2, 5 and 10. When finding the primes between 1 and 100 using the sieve method, check each instruction step by step to ensure that the correct numbers are struck out.

EXTENSION

Children should continue to use the same sieve method to find the prime numbers between 101 and 200. There are 21 of them. Encourage children to put forward their own theories about the properties of prime numbers and test them out. Introduce them to perfect numbers. These are numbers that are equal to the sum of their factors including 1 but excluding themselves. 6, for example, is a perfect number since 1 + 2 + 3 = 6. Which others can be found? Calculators may prove to be useful here.

NATIONAL NUMERACY STRATEGY LINKS

Year 4
Oral and mental starter

- Know by heart multiplication facts for 2, 3, 4, 5 and 10× tables.
- Begin to know multiplication facts for 6, 7, 8 and 9× tables.

Main teaching activity

- Recognise multiples of 2, 3, 4, 5 and 10, up to the tenth multiple.
- Explain methods and reasoning about numbers orally and in writing.
- Solve mathematical problems and puzzles.
- Recognise and explain patterns and relationships.
- Make and investigate a general statement about familiar numbers.
- Solve a problem by collecting quickly, organising, representing and interpreting data in Venn diagrams.

Year 6
Oral and mental starter

As Year 4 plus:

- Consolidate knowing by heart multiplication facts up to 10 × 10.
- Use factors when multiplying.

Main teaching activity

As Year 4 plus:

- Recognise multiples up to 10 × 10.
- Find simple common multiples.
- Recognise prime numbers to at least 20.
- Factorise numbers to 100 into prime factors.

6	216	690	724	427	66
74	172	474	274	114	144
924	294	492	220	372	86
108	218	308	87	168	612
96	408	384	78	999	432
4	409	406	774	666	444

7	37	903	609	546	665	840
35	497	679	906	78	588	200
28	433	297	84	693	336	574
97	392	455	385	654	217	777
802	602	583	99	260	321	28
198	861	100	504	378	63	287
19	742	763	49	197	123	77

● Travel through the maze from 6 to 66 using multiples of 6.

● This time travel from 7 to 77 using only mutiples of 7.

● In these empty squares make up your own number mazes.

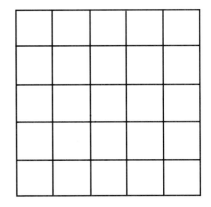

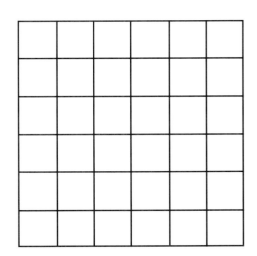

Use this 100 square to find all the prime numbers between 1 and 100.

1	2	3	4̸	5	6̸	7	8̸	9	1̸0̸
11	12	13	14	15	16	17	18	19	20
21	22	23	24	25	26	27	28	29	30
31	32	33	34	35	36	37	38	39	40
41	42	43	44	45	46	47	48	49	50
51	52	53	54	55	56	57	58	59	60
61	62	63	64	65	66	67	68	69	70
71	72	73	74	75	76	77	78	79	80
81	82	83	84	85	86	87	88	89	90
91	92	93	94	95	96	97	98	99	100

● Follow the instructions given in Chapter 1.

● List all the prime numbers here.

2

John Napier

Picking the bones out of multiplication

Like many people today, John Napier did not wish to spend too much of his valuable time working out mathematical calculations if there was a quicker way to find the answers.

Four hundred years ago, when Napier lived, the invention of electronic calculators and computers was still in the distant future. But after years of painstaking work using only simple materials, this resourceful man was able to develop special tables and a system of numbered rods to simplify multiplication and division.

Napier – born in 1550 – was a wealthy landowner who did not need to work for a living. He was born in a castle in the city of Edinburgh, Scotland, and the building remained the family home for the rest of his life. Napier studied at St Andrew's University when he was a teenager but his stay was short and he seems to have left without gaining any qualifications. Some time was then spent travelling abroad, as was the custom for wealthy young men in those days, but by the age of 21 he was back home in Scotland ready to concentrate on his chief hobby and interest – mathematics.

In 1614, after working on the system for some 20 years, Napier published his book *A Description of the Marvellous Rule of Logarithms*. This provided detailed tables of figures and described methods that could be used to multiply and divide large numbers quickly and easily. Soon afterwards followed another publication called *Rabdologia* in which Napier suggested the use of numbered rods to speed up the process of multiplication. These rods are often known as Napier's Bones because some of his earliest number columns were actually cut on bone.

Both of these systems seem very out of date today. But from them mathematicians developed the slide rule, a kind of mechanical calculator which continued to be used for detailed calculation work until it was replaced by cheap, small and easy-to-use electronic calculators.

Napier is also famous for pioneering the use of the decimal point in Britain. He may have come across the idea during his travels in Europe. He stressed the importance of using the point to separate whole numbers from fractions. The digits on the left of the decimal point would be the whole numbers while those on the right would be the fractional parts: tenths, hundredths, thousandths and so on.

As well as his discoveries and inventions in mathematics, Napier, who died in 1617 at the age of 67, also became closely involved in the political and religious affairs of Scotland at that time. A deeply religious man, he wrote several interpretations of the Bible and also took an active part in political affairs, especially the struggle between Protestants and Catholics.

There is also evidence that he had a more violent side to his nature. He spent some time designing weapons that could be used in the defence of his country. These included large mirrors that reflected the sun's rays in order to set fire to enemy equipment; new types of heavy guns; and a metal chariot which fired bullets through small holes in its wheels.

MEDIEVAL METHODS TO SIMPLIFY CALCULATIONS

Before looking in more detail at how to use Napier's Bones as an aid to multiplication, check that the children have a sound understanding of the multiplication and division processes and the close relationship between these two operations.

Multiplication is effectively repeated addition: 4×2 is a shorter and more convenient way of writing $2 + 2 + 2 + 2$, and 3×6 an alternative to $6 + 6 + 6$. Division can be seen as repeated subtraction. For example, in $20 \div 4$, taking one group of 4 away leaves 16 (20 – 4 = 16), taking two groups of 4 away leaves 12 (20 – 4 – 4 = 12), taking three groups of 4 away leaves 8 (20 – 4 – 4 – 4 = 8), taking four groups of 4 away leaves 4 (20 – 4 – 4 – 4 – 4 = 4) and taking the last group of 4 away leaves zero (20 – 4 – 4 – 4 – 4 – 4 = 0). From this we can say there are five groups of 4 in 20.

Also provide examples where multiplication and division are shown to be inverse operations of each other. These will not only help to establish important mathematical principles but also provide children with practical ways of checking that their calculations are correct. From the multiplication statement $3 \times 5 = 15$ we also know that $5 \times 3 = 15$, that $15 \div 5 = 3$ and that $15 \div 3 = 5$. If we start with the division statement $27 \div 9 = 3$ it is also true that $27 \div 3 = 9$, that $3 \times 9 = 27$ and that $9 \times 3 = 27$.

Children should be familiar with more traditional grid methods for multiplying numbers. These are based on a partition system with the tens and units or hundreds, tens and units being multiplied separately and then recombined through addition. Several examples are shown in Figure 2.1.

$$36 \times 4 = 30 \times 4 = 120$$
$$+ \; 6 \times 4 = \; \underline{24}$$
$$\underline{144}$$

$$127 \times 5 = 100 \times 5 = 500$$
$$+ \quad 20 \times 5 = 100$$
$$+ \quad \; 7 \times 5 = \; \underline{35}$$
$$\underline{635}$$

- **Figure 2.1:** Partition method

Napier's Bones

A set of Napier's Bones in the form of paper strips can be made by completing the boxes drawn on the photocopiable sheet at the end of this chapter. Mount the worksheet on to a thick piece of cardboard to add strength; a covering of clear plastic sheeting will prolong active life. Each number at the top is multiplied by each number on the side. The tens digit is always placed in the top left-hand corner and the units in the bottom right. Once the grid is complete, ask the children to cut along the vertical lines so they have a series of individual strips. To calculate 72×5, for example, lay the 7 and 2 strips alongside each other. Then add up numbers along the diagonals of the fifth line as shown by the arrows (Figure 2.2). Start on the right and work towards the left. If the totals make two digits, the tens should be carried on to the next diagonal. Try using larger numbers, for example 274×9 (Figure 2.3).

Gelosia (grating) method

An examination of Napier's Bones can be extended by challenging children to investigate the Gelosia or grating method of multiplying. This method was used in India from the twelfth century onwards, but also became popular in Europe later on. It is sometimes referred to as lattice multiplication because of the shape of the grids that are used.

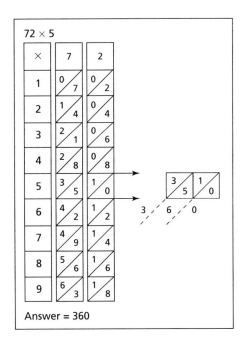

Answer = 360

• **Figure 2.2**

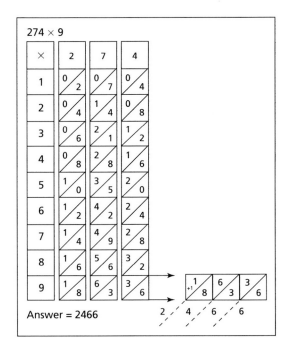

Answer = 2466

• **Figure 2.3**

To multiply 39 by 64 use squared paper complete with diagonal lines. Put 39 over the top two squares and 64 to the right of them. Fill in the squares in the same way as described before and add numbers in the diagonal lines. Again start on the right and carry where necessary (Figure 2.4). This process can also be used to multiply decimal numbers. Try 21.3 × 7.4 (Figure 2.5).

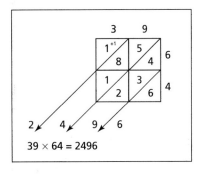

39 × 64 = 2496

• **Figure 2.4**

21·3 × 7·4 = 157·62

• **Figure 2.5**

There are other methods of multiplying numbers which children can try. They are often known by different names, which can be confusing, so titles have been avoided.

Method 1

Put down 1 on the left-hand side and the larger of the two numbers on the right. Keep doubling both sets of numbers until the number on the left is more than half the smaller number. Next, find the numbers on the left that total the smaller number. Cross out the other lines and add up those numbers that are left on the right (Figure 2.6).

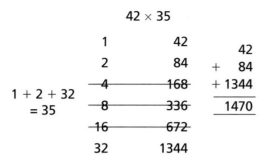

$$42 \times 35$$

1	42	42
2	84	+ 84
~~4~~	~~168~~	+ 1344
1 + 2 + 32		
= 35	~~8~~	~~336~~	1470
	~~16~~	~~672~~	
	32	1344	

• **Figure 2.6**

Method 2

Here, numbers on the left-hand side are doubled while those on the right are halved. Any remainders should not be included. When 1 is reached the process stops. Cross out all the rows which have an even number on the right-hand side and add those remaining on the left. Working out should be checked using a calculator (Figure 2.7).

$$56 \times 29$$

	56	29	
	~~112~~	~~14~~	even number
	224	7	
+	448	3	
	896	1	
	1624		

• **Figure 2.7**

Slide rule

A practical task children can carry out is the construction of a simple slide rule that can be used for further multiplication activities. Make the device using two strips of thick card. Mark them with divisions at 2 cm intervals and, as shown in Figure 2.8, double each number as they are written from left to right. To find the product of 4 and 8, for example, slide the upper strip along until 1 is opposite 4 on the lower strip. The answer, 32, can then be read off below 8 on the upper strip (Figure 2.9). Make strips marked with the powers of 3 as an alternative, that is 1, 3, 9, 27 and so on, and try other multiplication questions using this new slide rule.

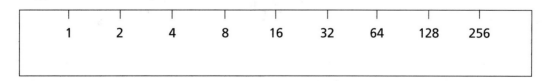

• **Figure 2.8**

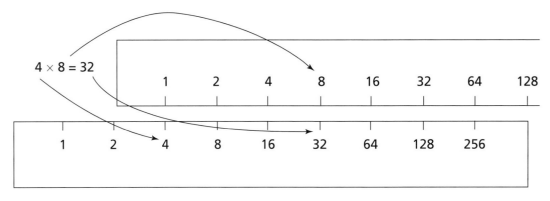

$4 \times 8 = 32$

| | 1 | 2 | 4 | 8 | 16 | 32 | 64 | 128 |

| | 1 | 2 | 4 | 8 | 16 | 32 | 64 | 128 | 256 |

• **Figure 2.9**

GETTING THE POINT

Washing line games

A good way to show both the importance and the versatility of the decimal point in our number system is to play washing line games. Peg the required numbers on the line using a set of digit cards 0–9 and a card showing the decimal point.

Start with tasks that involve just three digit cards and the point say, for example, 3, 7, 1 and the point. Invite volunteers out to peg up the correct answers on the washing line once questions have been asked. Key rules are that all four cards have to be used each time but that they cannot be used more than once in the same question.

Problems might include:

- What is the highest number that can be made? (731.)
- What is the smallest number? (.137)
- Which number is closest to 1? (.731)
- Which number is closest to 10? (7.31)
- What is the smallest number that can be made over 5? (7.13)
- What is the closest decimal number which can be made to 100? (73.1)

Calculators can be used to check that the solutions given are correct.

Square box method

As a variation to adding decimal numbers in the traditional way, try the square box method. In Figure 2.10 the two decimal numbers in the top row have been added together and the answer placed in the right-hand square. Repeat the process with the centre row. Then add the two decimal numbers in the left-hand column and fill in the answer in the bottom left-hand square. Do the same with the centre column. To complete the square, add the numbers in the bottom row and the right-hand column. If the addition has been done correctly, the same total should be produced and this should be written into the answer box at the bottom on the right.

Ask children to complete other 3×3 squares to see if the same pattern occurs. What is the result if 4×4 squares are used instead? Another problem-solving activity involving decimal numbers is given on the photocopiable sheet *Decimal flowers*.

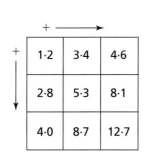

1·2	3·4	4·6
2·8	5·3	8·1
4·0	8·7	12·7

1·5	2·3	6·7	10·5
3·0	4·7	2·8	10·5
6·9	5·8	4·1	16·8
11·4	12·8	13·6	37·8

● **Figure 2.10**

SUPPORT

Again, because of the amount of multiplying involved some children will need to rely heavily on table squares. Ensure that the children have a sound grasp of TU × U before introducing higher numbers. Encourage them to check questions like this by using the partition method; for example, 26 × 4 = 20 × 4 + 6 × 4 = 80 + 24 = 104. When introducing decimals, focus on work with tenths first and reinforce concepts by linking tasks closely to money (£1.20) and metric units (1.5 metres).

EXTENSION

With a number of different methods of multiplication at their disposal, children should be able to work the same questions in a number of different ways to see if they produce the same answers. Try this investigation to sharpen up their skills. The squares and rectangles in Figure 2.11 have been taken from a completed multiplication square up to 10 × 10. What answers are produced when the numbers in the opposite corners are multiplied? Does the same thing happen with all squares and rectangles drawn inside the square? Solutions can be checked with a calculator. Encourage the children to work with numbers to two decimal places as soon as they are ready.

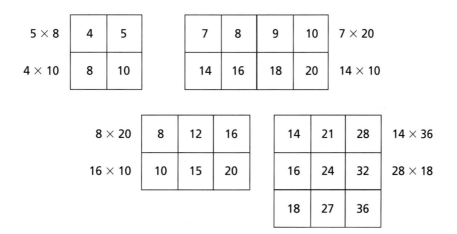

● **Figure 2.11:** Boxes from table square

Multiply, times, product, multiplied, multiplication, division, repeated addition, repeated subtraction, double, halve, decimal number, decimal point, decimal fraction, decimal place, tenth, hundredth, thousandth, digit, partition, inverse operation.

Thick card, clear plastic covering, scissors, glue, squared paper (1 cm and 2 cm), digit cards 0–9 and decimal point, washing line, pegs, calculators, photocopiable pages 24 and 25.

NATIONAL NUMERACY STRATEGY LINKS

Year 4
Oral and mental starter

- Know by heart multiplication facts for 2, 3, 4, 5 and 10× tables.
- Begin to know multiplication facts for 6, 7, 8 and 9× tables.
- Derive quickly doubles for all numbers to 50 and doubles of multiples of 10 to 500 and the corresponding halves.
- Use doubling or halving starting from known facts.

Main teaching activity

- Extend understanding of the operations of × and ÷ and their relationship to each other and also + and −.
- Develop and refine written methods of TU × U.
- Check calculations with the inverse operation.
- Understand decimal notation and place value for tenths and hundredths and use in context.

Year 6
Oral and mental starter

As Year 4 plus:

- Consolidate knowing by heart multiplication facts up to 10 x 10.
- Use related facts when doubling or halving.
- Doubles of two-digit numbers.
- Derive quickly doubles of multiples of 10 to 1,000.
  Doubles of multiples of 100 to 10,000 and the corresponding halves.

Main teaching activity

As Year 4 plus:

- Extend written methods to ThHTU x U.
- Multiplication of a three-digit integer by a two-digit integer.
- Multiplication of numbers involving decimals.
- Developing and using calculator skills.
- Use decimal notation for tenths and hundredths in calculations.

X	2	3	4	5	6	7	8	9
1	0 / 2	0 / 3	0 / 4	0 / 5	0 / 6	0 / 7	0 / 8	0 / 9
2	0 / 4	0 / 6	0 / 8	1 / 0				
3	0 / 6	0 / 9	1 / 2					
4	0 / 8							
5								
6								
7								
8								
9								

Complete the boxes to make the number strips.

<u>Remember</u>: The tens digit goes in the top left-hand corner, the units in the bottom right.

DECIMAL FLOWERS

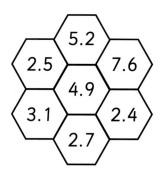

In this decimal flower two of the petal numbers can be added to make 2.7 and two of the petal numbers can be subtracted to make 2.7

eg.   2.5 + 2.4 = 4.9
      7.6 – 2.7 = 4.9

Find the totals and differences to make the centre number of these decimal flowers:

1

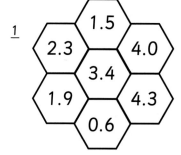

3

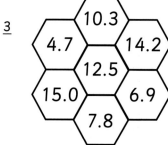

2

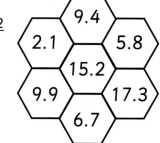

4

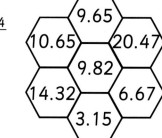

Make up some decimal flowers of your own.

family had moved from Clermont-Ferrand to Paris in 1630 following the death of Pascal's mother. Pascal was always a quick learner, especially as his father believed that no new subject should be taught until the previous one had been mastered.

As an adult, Pascal was always keen to link his expertise in maths with his interest in science. One of his first inventions was a mechanical calculator, which was really a type of adding machine. He hoped his father would be able to use this to work out difficult accounts.

In science, he became fascinated with air pressure and it is from his work on this subject that many pieces of equipment we use today developed. These include: the barometer – used in weather forecasting; the syringe; and the type of braking system found in heavy goods vehicles like lorries and buses. His most important discovery on this subject is called Pascal's Law. It says that liquids give out pressure equally in all directions and that any alteration in pressure at one point will cause identical changes elsewhere.

Working with another famous French mathematician called Pierre de Fermat, Pascal put forward important ideas about the theory of probability – the likelihood of an event actually taking place. He studied the occurrence of unusual happenings such as accidents, equipment breakdowns and bad weather conditions. Some of his theories are still used today by businesses such as insurance companies which study the record of claims made in the past to forecast what might happen in the future. They are, of course, only theories, so they often turn out to be wrong.

The arithmetical triangle to which Pascal gave his name had been known for many years but he discovered that many of its properties were linked to certain number series and sequences, including those worked on by people like Leonardo Fibonacci 400 years earlier.

In later life, Pascal abandoned his work in science and maths and devoted the rest of his time to writing about religion. In 1654 he joined a religious group called the Jansenists and spent the last eight years of his life in a community run by them at Port Royal. Many of his religious writings were published after his death in 1662 when he was only 39. Pascal tried to apply his theories on probability to his views on religion. He argued that even though trying to find perfect happiness was extremely difficult, if not impossible, people who attempted to lead a good Christian life stood more chance of finding it than those who behaved differently or had other beliefs.

TRIANGULAR NUMBER PATTERNS

To build up the number series known as Pascal's Triangle it is necessary to start each row with 1 and end each row with 1. In between, numbers are found by adding adjacent numbers above the space (Figure 3.1). Children should keep increasing the size of the triangle until it reaches the stage shown on the photocopiable sheet at the end of this chapter. It does not have to stop there, and some groups of children may wish to continue. A calculator will speed up the addition once the numbers increase in size.

Encourage investigation into how the triangle has been made and what its properties are. What kind of pattern is made when the numbers are totalled across the line? Does this pattern continue if the triangle is extended? Examine the patterns formed by adding diagonal lines within the triangle. Look at 1, 2, 3, 4, 5; 1, 3, 6, 10; 1, 4, 10, 20, for example.

The triangle as a shape provides the basis for other interesting number challenges. In Figure 3.2 the patterns are produced by applying the rule found in Pascal's Triangle in reverse. In this case, two adjacent numbers are added to make the number that comes above them, not below. Easy starter examples are shown, but by increasing the triangles in size and changing the location of the numbers given, more complex problems can be devised. This is also another excellent method for improving expertise in the addition of decimal numbers. The patterns in Figure 3.3 are made using alternate numbers, odd or even, or consecutive numbers. Here, the children should be shown how the pattern starts and then left to investigate its development.

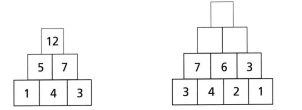
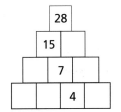

● **Figure 3.2:** Pyramid numbers

Even	Odd	Consecutive
2 = 2	1 = 1	1 = 1
2 + 4 = 6	1 + 3 = 4	1 + 2= 3
2 + 4 + 6 = 12	1 + 3 + 5 = 9	1 + 2+ 3 = 6
2 + 4 + 6 + 8 = 20	1 + 3 + 5 + 7 = 16	1 + 2+ 3+ 4 = 10

● **Figure 3.3**

Triangular numbers

The family actually known as triangular numbers can be formed diagrammatically in several different ways. These are shown in Figure 3.4. Look closely first at the differences between triangular numbers 1, 3, 6, 10 and so on. Then predict how the sequence will develop so there will no longer be the need to actually draw the

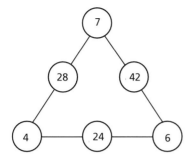

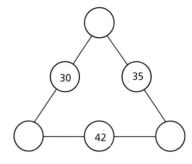

● **Figure 3.9:** Multiplication triangle   ● **Figure 3.10:** Multiplication triangle

children will need to find the numbers to fit into the three corner positions (Figure 3.10). This activity will improve children's multiplication of single-digit numbers and help them with their recognition of multiples and factors.

Another triangular pattern activity to try out is on the photocopiable sheet *Ups and downs*. Using isometric grid paper, draw the shapes that are shown. Continue the pattern by shading the correct number of small triangles and leaving the others blank. Carry on the process, increasing the size of the large triangle and following the same pattern of shading. Then complete the table. Look down the columns and investigate the number patterns which begin to emerge. Where have these sequences been seen before and to which special families do they belong?

WHAT ARE THE CHANCES?

All of us live in a world in which the outcomes of some events are certain while others are more unpredictable. If a ball is thrown into the air it will certainly come back down to earth as the law of gravity determines this. But, on the other hand, while we know for sure that the sun will rise tomorrow, we cannot be absolutely certain whether it will be foggy, sunny, cloudy or rainy. Probability and its connection with the gathering of statistics is an important area of mathematics and one with which children should be familiar. Practical work on its own, though, is not sufficient and children should always be encouraged to talk about what they are doing, how they are going to record their results and what they have found out.

Discuss first of all the concepts of impossible and certain. On a simple probability scale, if an outcome is impossible then the probability of this happening is 0. If an outcome is certain, then the probability of this happening is 1. All other probabilities lie somewhere between these two numbers and can be recorded on the scale.

Tossing coins

Start with an activity where there are only two possible outcomes. Tossing a coin is a simple experiment that is easy to organise. Establish first that when a coin is tossed it is equally likely to come down heads or tails. This is what is known as an even chance. Working with a partner, children should then predict how many heads and how many tails they would expect to get if the coin was tossed ten times. What result might be expected if the number of tosses was increased to 20, 50, or 100? Theories should then be tested out and the results recorded accurately. How close to their predictions were the results and did the number of tosses significantly effect their findings?

Throwing dice

Move on to increase the number of possible outcomes. Mark a blank dice with small circles on two of the faces. Mark a small square on just one face and leave the remaining three faces blank. Through discussion the children should be able to tell you that the chances of throwing a blank face is most likely because there are three of them out of the total of six faces. They should also be able to predict that the chance of throwing a square is least likely because there is only one of them. The likelihood of the circle coming face up will lie somewhere between these two.

Using squared paper and the initial letters B (blank), C (circle), and S (square) should enable children to keep count of their throws and also speed up the recording process. From 60 throws the expected outcome might be 30 blanks, 20 circles and 10 squares but the main discussion point will revolve around how closely these predictions match the children's actual results.

Predicting

Finally, place eight counters into a bag. Five should be coloured red, two blue and one green. This time, encourage the children to think of the possible outcomes in terms of fractions. They may be able to predict that the chances of pulling out a red counter will be five-eighths, a blue counter two-eighths and the green only one-eighth. They should also be challenged to suggest the number of times they will need to pull out a counter in order to get as close as possible to this result.

Ask them to test out their ideas, always remembering to replace the counter each time it has taken been out. Suggest this time that studying the combined results of all the groups in the class might provide the kind of large sample needed to produce a more accurate conclusion. Hopefully they will come to appreciate that the larger the number of results collected, the more likelihood there is of getting closer to the ratio 5:2:1.

Support

Give help and advice when number patterns and sequences are being investigated. Use parts of sequences where the numbers are lower and the pattern easier to spot. Some may need to be almost completed with gaps left for the children to fill in. In activities like balanced triangles, provide most of the numbers needed, leaving children to calculate missing numbers by making totals and then working out differences. Work with children during probability tasks, assisting them with the testing of ideas and the methods used for recording. Express findings in simple terms after thorough discussion.

PASCAL'S TRIANGLE ACTIVITY SHEET

Look at this triangle. Work out how it is made and fill in the missing numbers.

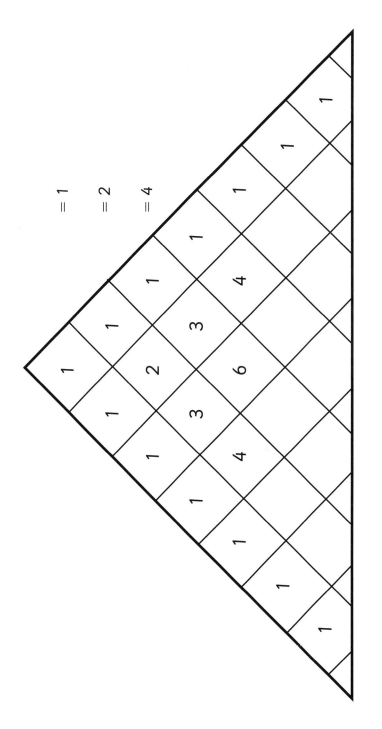

= 1

= 2

= 4

- Add the numbers across the line. Find the pattern in these numbers.
- Look for other patterns in these numbers. Look closely at the diagonal lines.

UPS AND DOWNS

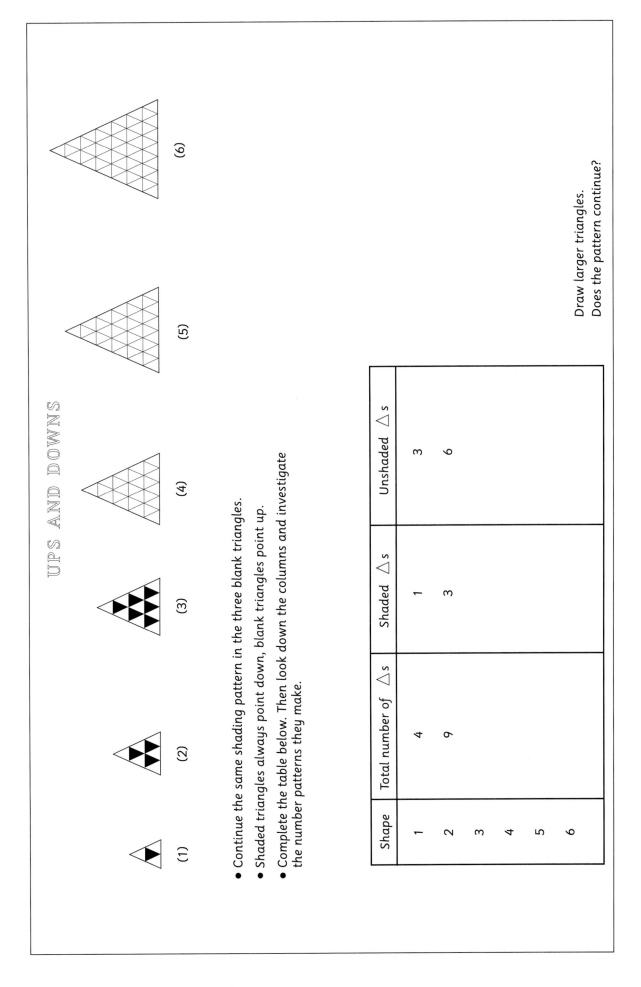

(1)   (2)   (3)   (4)   (5)   (6)

- Continue the same shading pattern in the three blank triangles.
- Shaded triangles always point down, blank triangles point up.
- Complete the table below. Then look down the columns and investigate the number patterns they make.

Shape	Total number of △s	Shaded △s	Unshaded △s
1	4	1	3
2	9	3	6
3			
4			
5			
6			

Draw larger triangles.
Does the pattern continue?

North Africa. During his travels he came into contact with number systems which had started in India and methods of calculating that had been perfected by the Arabs. He became particularly good at working out the profit margins that traders would be able to make buying and selling and also the rates of exchange between the different money systems they used. For a time he studied with an Arab teacher who helped him to improve his computing techniques and also introduced him to the work of classical mathematicians such as Euclid and Pythagoras.

Fibonacci is best known for his sequence of numbers that was first described in his book *Liber Abaci* or *The Book of Calculations*. This was published in 1202 and was the first book in Europe to merge together mathematical ideas from India and the Arab world.

In the Fibonacci sequence, each number is the sum of the previous two (0, 1, 1, 2, 3, 5, 8, 13 and so on). The sequence can be observed in many natural situations, such as the arrangement of leaves on a flower stem, the spiral pattern on a snail shell and the segments in a pineapple or pine cone. Sunflower heads, for example, contain seeds set in spirals, with 21 spirals clockwise and 34 spirals anticlockwise. Both of these are consecutive numbers in the Fibonacci sequence. Pine cones and pineapples have eight seeds in their clockwise spirals and 13 in those going anticlockwise. The number of petals found on many flowers also feature in the sequence. Buttercups have five petals, for example, some marigolds 13 and members of the daisy family 34, 55 or 89. During times of war, when it has become important to be able to send secret messages, the Fibonacci sequence has often been used as the basis for codes and ciphers.

In another of his publications, Fibonacci looked at the importance of square numbers and he also wrote about other mathematical topics such as geometry, proportion and the roots of equations. Although the word zero comes from a Latin word meaning empty or blank, it was Fibonacci in *Liber Abaci* who stressed its importance. Many number systems in the ancient world did not use a zero and for this reason calculations often became very complex. This extra digit, Fibonacci argued, was necessary as a place or position holder, separating columns of figures and making the difference, for example, between numbers like 172, 1072, 1702 and 1720.

It is believed that Fibonacci died in about 1250 when he was in his eighties. There are records in Pisa which show that later in life he was paid an annual salary by the city. This may have been because they recognised him as an important figure of his time. Or perhaps it was a way of thanking him for his help with the financial administration of the city.

NATURE'S NUMBER PATTERN

The Fibonacci sequence of numbers has been started on the photocopiable sheet at the end of this chapter. Continue with the sequence as far as the sheet will allow and then start to examine it in more detail.

First, draw a line under any number in the line. The total of all the numbers above the line should be equal to one less than the second number below it. For example, put a line under 34 then check to see if the rule is true.

Move on to try other possibilities. For instance, take any three numbers in sequence. Try low numbers like 2, 3 and 5 to start with. Square the middle number – 3 squared is equal to 9 – and multiply the first and third numbers together (the product of 2 and 5 is 10). Discuss what is significant about the difference between the two answers. Try this a number of times. Is the difference always the same? (See Figure 4.1.)

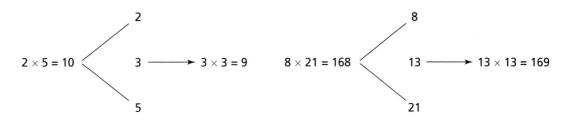

Square middle number; multiply outside numbers.

• **Figure 4.1**

Number trick

Now ask the children to try this number trick. It should work every time because in the Fibonacci series the seventh number is always one-eleventh of the total of the first ten numbers. Working in pairs, one of them writes down the first number in a block of ten squares. Ask the second child to put down another number in the second place. The series is then continued, adding the last two numbers together each time. When the seventh number is reached, the first child multiplies it by 11 but keeps the answer a secret. The other child completes the sequence of ten numbers and then adds them all together using a calculator to check if necessary. Check that the predicted answer matches (Figure 4.2).

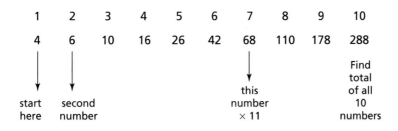

$68 \times 11 = 748$
Total of all ten numbers = 748

• **Figure 4.2**

Investigations

● Look again at the numbers in the sequence. Take any two consecutive numbers and work out the difference between them. Write down the answers. Move along to the next number and do this again. Continue the process. What pattern of numbers has been produced (Figure 4.3)?

reading, marking the point where positive numbers change to negative ones. Show the children some examples of measuring devices that have a zero on their scales.

Return to the activity suggested in Chapter 2 on John Napier, where a washing line and digit cards were used to consolidate work on decimal notation. Initially discard the decimal point and use four digits, one of which should be a zero. Stress the important differences it makes in place value as you ask children to peg up certain numbers. If the 5, 0, 7, 1 cards are used, ask questions like the following:

- What is the highest number that can be made? (7510)
- What is the smallest number using all four cards? (1057 as 157 would not normally be written as 0157)
- Which number would be closest to 2000? (1750)
- Which number would be closest to 5000? (5017)

Then allow the children free access to any digit cards they want to use and also include a decimal point. Ask one of them to put up a decimal number, for example, 0.38. Add 1 to this number (1.38). Ask another child to make it 10 more (10.38). Can someone else make it 100 more (100.38)? What would happen if the starting number was made ten times more (3.8)? Or ten times smaller (0.038)?

SQUARE NUMBERS

Ensure first that the children can recognise all the square numbers up to 100 by drawing the shapes on squared paper, as shown in Figure 4.7. They should also be aware of the range of vocabulary that is used to describe this process: for example:

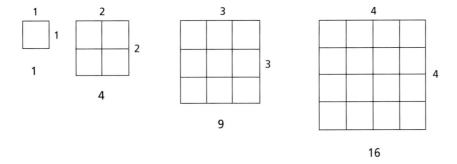

- **Figure 4.7:** Square numbers

- What is 3 squared?
- What is the square of 5?
- Which number multiplied by itself gives 49?
- What is the area of a square whose sides are 9 cm in length?
- What is 6 to the power of 2?

Look then at the differences between the square numbers to see what pattern can be established (Figure 4.8). Also investigate the way square numbers can be calculated by adding consecutive numbers up to the number being squared and then back down to 1 again. For example, 3 squared can be found by adding 1 + 2 + 3 + 2 +1 = 9, and 5 squared would be 1 + 2 + 3 + 4 + 5 + 4 + 3 + 2 + 1 = 25.

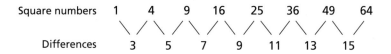

Square numbers   1   4   9   16   25   36   49   64

Differences   3   5   7   9   11   13   15

● **Figure 4.8**

Finally, using the square numbers between 1 and 100, can the children find a pair of square numbers that can be added or subtracted to make each of the numbers between 1 and 20: 1 + 1 = 2, 16 – 9 = 7, 36 – 25 = 11, but which others can be made and are there any which are not possible?

SUPPORT

When working with the Fibonacci sequence of numbers, base activities around the lower numbers so that calculations can be carried out more easily. The investigations will still work. Calculators will be needed to check answers when the numbers become larger. When pairs work is being carried out, ask children to assist each other in the computational process. Encourage the use of coins when carrying out the money investigation. Use centimetre squared paper to keep spiral designs accurate. Use only two digit cards in addition to the zero when making numbers for the washing line. Make sure small internal squares are counted up carefully to reinforce the understanding of square numbers.

EXTENSION

The Fibonacci sequence should be taken as far as the children are able to go. It will make their investigations more relevant if theories are tested on a larger sample of numbers. Once an identifiable pattern has been found in an answer, encourage the children to predict what will happen next as soon as possible. Their ideas should then be tested out. Ask them to work in pairs with large pieces of squared paper to continue to increase the size of the spiral drawing. In the number chains task, suggest the use of two- and three-digit numbers, mixed numbers and decimal numbers. Try this activity: using a calculator, reduce 968.25 to zero by subtracting five numbers (–900, –60, –8, –0.2, –0.05). Take 375.92 back to zero in five steps and 356.298 back to zero in six moves.

KEY VOCABULARY

Sequence, series, pattern, rule, method, strategy, continue, predict, test, square number, consecutive number, spiral, clockwise, anti-clockwise, number chain, zero, digit, decimal number, decimal place, decimal point, multiplied by itself, squared, power of, calculator, display, key, enter, clear, operation.

```
RESOURCES

    1p and 2p coins, squared paper, coloured pens, weighing scales, measuring
    tapes, thermometer, washing line, pegs, digit cards plus decimal point,
    calculators, photocopiable pages 47 and 48.
```

NATIONAL NUMERACY STRATEGY LINKS

Year 4
Oral and mental starters

- Add three or four small numbers.
- Use known number facts and place value to add or subtract mentally, including any pair of two-digit numbers.
- Partition into tens and units, adding the tens first.

Main teaching activity

- Read and write whole numbers to at least 10,000 in figures and words and know what each digit represents.
- Recognise and extend number sequences.
- Understand decimal notation and place value for tenths and hundredths.
- Choose and use appropriate number operations and appropriate ways of calculating.
- Explain methods and reasoning about numbers.
- Solve mathematical problems or puzzles.
- Recognise and explain patterns and relationships, generalise and predict.

Year 6
Oral and mental starters

As Year 4 plus:

- Add several numbers.
- Use known number facts to consolidate mental addition/subtraction.
- Use known number facts and place value to consolidate mental multiplication and division.

Main teaching activity

As Year 4 plus:

- Multiply and divide decimals mentally.
- Recognise squares of numbers to at least 12 x 12.
- Know what each digit represents in a number with up to three decimal places.
- Suggest extensions to mathematical problems and puzzles asking 'What if . . .?'.

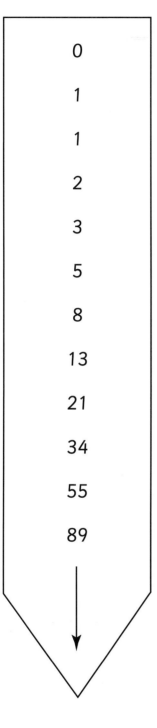

Almost 800 years ago the
Italian, Leonardo Fibonacci,
created this number sequence.
Each number is made by
adding the two numbers which
come before it.
Continue the line as far as you can.
Then use the line for the
activities described in Chapter 4.

3	6	9	15	24

In the boxes above you get each number by adding the previous two numbers. For example, 3 + 6 = 9, 6 + 9 = 15, 9 + 15 = 24.

Complete these boxes using the same rule:

3	1			

9		20		

5			17	

	12			52

			35	60

1				$12\frac{1}{2}$

Make up some number chains of your own.

5
René Descartes
Thinking your way to the solution

Descartes believed that the most important activity any person could do was to think. He was so convinced of this belief that on most days of his adult life he would lie in bed until eleven o'clock reading and meditating. In fact, a sudden change to this habit was to have tragic consequences, as we shall see later in his story.

This Frenchman, who was born near Tours in 1596, was not only a brilliant scientist and mathematician, he is often called the father of modern philosophy – the word means the search for wisdom and knowledge. Trying to unravel the nature of existence, Descartes originated the famous phrase *Cogito ergo sum*. It means 'I think, therefore I am', and was his way of explaining that he was certain he existed because he was able to think.

In his famous and most widely read book, *Discourse on Method*, he provided useful advice for anyone trying to solve a problem, especially in mathematics. He wrote about the four rules that should be followed in order to reach a solution. First, nothing should be accepted as being true unless it is absolutely clear that it is so. Second, it is better to solve a problem by looking at it step by step. Third, solutions are easier to find if we start with simple matters and gradually move to things that are more complicated. Finally, it is important at the end of a problem-solving situation to review thoroughly what has been found out in order to make sure that nothing has been missed.

Descartes' formal education started at the age of eight when he began to attend a church school run by Jesuit priests at La Flèche. He studied there for eight years before moving to the University of Poitiers, where he took a course in law. He qualified in 1616 but never actually took up a position as a lawyer. His family and friends encouraged him to become a Member of Parliament but, as he would have had to wait seven years until he reached the age of 27 to do this, he soon lost interest.

So, at his own expense, he became a soldier, not because he was really interested in fighting but as a way of travelling easily throughout Europe and also because he claimed it gave him the time to think. Between 1618 and 1628 he visited many countries including Holland, Germany and Italy where, as he said later, he was able to 'study the book of the world'.

In 1628, after selling the property he still owned in France, he returned to Holland and lived there quietly thinking and writing until 1649. His writings on geometry did much to convert the work of Euclid and other Greek scholars into a form we can understand today. He introduced the letters x and y into mathematics, to represent variables, and the symbols + and – for addition and subtraction. Cartesian co-ordinates, which are used to plot positions on a grid, are named after him although he never used this method himself. Descartes also invented the use of indices to express the powers of numbers. He studied astronomy and in science put forward theories about the circulation of the blood and the movement of light.

This learned man might have lived longer than his 54 years if he had not gone to Stockholm, the capital of Sweden, in 1649. Descartes moved there to give lessons in philosophy to Queen Christina. But, despite his usual habit of rising late, she insisted that teaching should start at five o'clock in the morning three times each week. It was here in the following year that, unused to such early mornings in a very cold climate, he caught pneumonia and died.

FIRST ON THE GRID

In the method of using algebra in geometry developed by Descartes, a pair of numbers taken from two axes can be used to represent a fixed point. The two axes meet at a right angle and zero is the point where the axes cross. When writing the co-ordinates, (3,5) for example, the first number represents the distance along the horizontal (x) axis and the second shows the distance along the vertical (y) axis.

Plotting co-ordinates

Children should carry out the task provided on the photocopiable sheet *What shapes have been made?*. Remind them that the horizontal number always comes first and that it is important that the points are joined with straight lines in the order they are given. What shapes have been made by plotting the points?

They should then be encouraged to make their own two-dimensional shapes on squared paper using the same form of grid system. Let them work in pairs, with one child devising points for the other to plot. Results can then be swapped. To make repeated shapes or more intricate patterns, ask the children to plot matching positions in a second, third and fourth quadrant (Figure 5.1). This provides the potential for the use of negative numbers and the chance to produce shapes that have several lines of reflective symmetry.

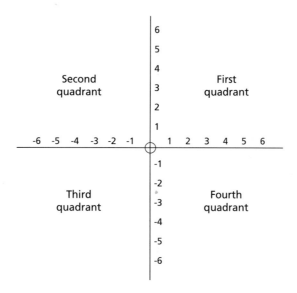

• **Figure 5.1**

Also investigate what happens when changes are made to the co-ordinates used to plot a simple picture. Plot these co-ordinates on a 10 × 10 grid, joining the points in the order they are given: (6,2), (4,2), (4,5), (1,5), (5,9), (9,5), (6,5), (6,2).

- What happens if the first co-ordinate is doubled?
- What happens if the second co-ordinate is doubled? What happens if both co-ordinates are doubled?
- What happens if the co-ordinates are reversed?

Plotting linked to movement

Move on to try plotting positions linked with movement. It is best to use dotty paper this time. Figure 5.2 shows how to start plotting a repeated set of digits. In this example, 233 has been used. It should be continued until the shape is complete (Figure 5.3). It is important that these rules are followed throughout. The first move should always be to the right. A turn is made for each new digit, going 90 degrees clockwise. The digit 3 does not mean linking three dots; it means drawing a straight line between the dots through three spaces. Sometimes lines may go over ones previously drawn.

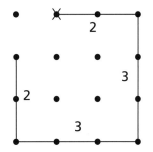

Figure 5.2: Start of 233 pattern

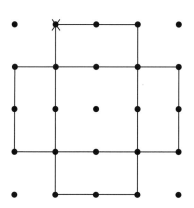

Figure 5.3: Completed 233 pattern

Experiment with other patterns. Try 123, 263 and 342. Is an identical shape produced if the same digits are rearranged in a different order? Check with 124, 241 and 412. It is said that many four-digit patterns produce open designs that do not return to their starting point. Examine this theory by using 2113 and 3211.

MAKING GRAPHS

Times tables can also be plotted using the types of grids mentioned at the beginning. In Figure 5.4, the numbers of the six times table (0, 6 12, 18, 24, 30 and so on) have been plotted using the first digit on the horizontal (x) axis and the second digit on the vertical (y) axis. How does the pattern compare with those made by other tables plotted in this way? Look at the 4×, 8× and 10× tables, for example.

Also explore the type of constant proportion graph which is formed if numbers are plotted as shown in Figure 5.5:

- Why is a straight line produced this time?
- Why does the line originate from zero?
- Can the children explain why this is known as constant proportion?
- Do all the times tables respond in this way?

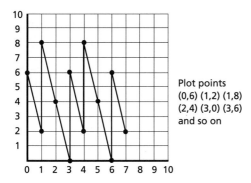

Plot points
(0,6) (1,2) (1,8)
(2,4) (3,0) (3,6)
and so on

- **Figure 5.4:** 6× table

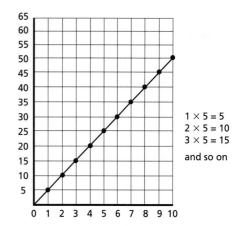

1 × 5 = 5
2 × 5 = 10
3 × 5 = 15

and so on

- **Figure 5.5:** Table graph of 5× table

Extend the children's investigations of graphs to those that are made using curves as opposed to straight lines. These enable us to take readings once the original points have been plotted. Figure 5.6 shows a graph of the square numbers between 1 and 10. Remind the children that when you square a number you multiply it by itself. Once 1, 4, 9, 16 and so on have been plotted and the graph drawn, the children should be able to find the squares of 4½, 6½ and 9½ accurately without using calculators. Ask them to suggest what other forms of data could be shown on a curved line graph like this.

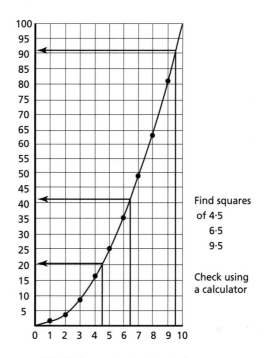

Find squares
of 4·5
    6·5
    9·5

Check using
a calculator

- **Figure 5.6:** Graph of the square numbers from 1 to 10

POSITIVE AND NEGATIVE INTEGERS

A line of integers with a difference is shown on the photocopiable sheet *Positive (+) and negative (-)*. Here, numbers on the right-hand side of the line are positive numbers. They carry the + sign. Numbers on the left-hand side of the line are negative numbers and carry the – sign. Starting at –2 and jumping five spaces in a positive direction would mean landing on +3, while starting on +4 and jumping seven spaces in a negative direction would mean landing on –3.

Carry out similar jumping tasks and also activities where both positive and negative numbers have to be placed in order of size. This will help the children to move along the line with greater confidence. For example, put these numbers in order of size starting with the smallest: –6, 4, –3, 0, 12, –1. Before the children start to work this sheet, explain to them that this is the number line which is also found on thermometers and that some of the questions deal with the reading of temperatures. Point out that temperatures below zero are normally differentiated by the word minus and not negative: for example, a temperature 5 degrees below zero is said to be minus 5 and not negative 5.

INDEX NUMBERS

An index number is always written on the upper right of a number to show how many times that number has been multiplied by itself. We show 4 squared ($4 \times 4 = 16$) in two dimensions by writing 4^2. A cube is in three dimensions: it has length, width and height. It takes 64 small cubes to make a cube with faces $4 \times 4 \times 4$ (Figure 5.7). 4 to the third power, or 4 cubed, is 64. Ask the children to work out 3 cubed. And what is 5 to the power of 3?

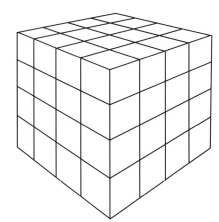

• **Figure 5.7**

We cannot draw the fourth dimension in diagrams, but we can use it to calculate numbers. So $2 \times 2 \times 2 \times 2$ or 2^4 equals 16. A number with the index 1 is always the number itself: for example, 4^1, or 4 to the power of 1, is equal to 4. A number with the index 0 is always equal to 1. So 4^0 or 4 to the power of 0 is equal to 1.

Make an index counting board like the one shown in Figure 5.8 and look for a pattern in the right-hand column. Draw other index counting boards for other

Index counting board		
3^0		1
3^1	3	3
3^2	3×3	9
3^3	$3 \times 3 \times 3$	
3^4		
3^5		
3^6		

● **Figure 5.8:** Index counting board

numbers such as 3, 4 and 5 and ask the children to find the highest power that they can calculate.

Talk about how useful index numbers were before calculators became common, particularly when using large numbers. 10^6 was so much easier and quicker to write than $10 \times 10 \times 10 \times 10 \times 10 \times 10$ or 1,000,000.

Discuss with the children how other members of the tens family would be written using index notation. Give them the part of the table shown in Figure 5.9 and ask them to complete the rest. While talking of big numbers, see if they can solve these problems:

Complete the table:

1×10	10×10	___ $\times 10$	1000×10	___ $\times 10$	$100,000 \times 10$
10	100	1000	_____	100,000	
10^1	___	10^3	10^4	___	___

● **Figure 5.9**

● Have you lived for one million minutes?
● Would it be possible to walk one million millimetres during a day?
● Do you drink one million millilitres in one year?
● If you were given one million pence, how much would they be worth in pounds?

Stress that they must be able to explain the strategies they have used to find their solutions, and that they should record their working out.

SUPPORT

Help will be needed when drawing up grids to make sure that axes are correctly positioned and that lines are numbered instead of spaces. Use grids for making simple 2D shapes like triangles, squares and rectangles. Ensure that points are joined in the correct sequence. Symmetrical shapes should be made using only two quadrants initially. Use multiplication charts to help with the accurate construction of table graphs. Practice in jumping around on more traditional number lines will be necessary before the introduction of positive and negative numbers. Use small interlocking cubes to construct models of square and cube numbers, for example, 3 squared (3×3) and 2 cubed ($2 \times 2 \times 2$).

EXTENSION

Encourage the children to construct more complicated 2D shapes on the grids, such as rhombus, trapezium and other members of the quadrilateral family, pentagon and hexagon. Use all four quadrants for symmetrical shapes and patterns, possibly rotating the shape from one quadrant to another. The children should devise their own repeated digit sequences to link position and movement. When table graph patterns have been drawn, compare results. Check similarities between 2, 4, and 8, for example, or between 5 and 10. The children should suggest their own ideas for making curved line graphs. Use a thermometer, particularly during the wintertime, to collect real data involving positive and negative numbers and investigate the best ways of recording the temperatures.

KEY VOCABULARY

Position, direction, plot, grid, row, column, origin, zero, co-ordinates, straight line, horizontal, vertical, x axis, y axis, quadrant, rotate, degree, 2D, two-dimensional, quadrilateral, rhombus, trapezium, pentagon, hexagon, symmetrical, line of symmetry, reflective symmetry, graph, constant proportion, temperature, thermometer, integer, positive, negative, minus, above/below zero, index number, index notation, power of.

RESOURCES

Squared paper, multiplication charts, plastic mirrors, thermometers, positive/negative number lines, interlocking cubes, calculators, photocopiable pages 58 and 59.

NATIONAL NUMERACY STRATEGY LINKS

Year 4
Oral and mental starter

- Know by heart multiplication facts for 2, 3, 4, 5 and 10× tables.
- Begin to know multiplication facts for 6, 7, 8 and 9× tables.
- Derive quickly division facts corresponding to 2, 3, 4, 5 and 10× tables.

Main teaching activity

- Read and write whole numbers to at least 10,000.
- Recognise negative numbers in context.
- Solve a problem by collecting quickly, organising, representing and interpreting data in tables, charts, graphs and diagrams.
- Describe and visualise 2D shapes.
- Make shapes and discuss properties such as lines of symmetry.
- Recognise positions and directions; for example, describe and find the position of a point on a grid of squares where the lines are numbered.

Year 6
Oral and mental starter

As Year 4 plus:

- Consolidate knowing by heart multiplication facts up to 10×10.
- Derive quickly division facts corresponding to tables up to 10×10.

Main teaching activity

As Year 4 plus:

- Find the difference between a positive and a negative integer, or two negative integers, in a context such as temperature or the number line, and order a set of positive and negative integers.
- Solve a problem by extracting and interpreting data in tables, graphs and charts.
- Classify quadrilaterals.
- Make shapes with increasing accuracy.
- Recognise where a shape will be after two translations.
- Read and plot co-ordinates in all four quadrants.

6
Archimedes
Putting ideas into action

It is a tragedy worthy of the Greeks that one of the most eminent scientists and mathematicians of the ancient world should lose his life because of a chance remark.

The story is told that after the Romans had captured the city of Syracuse in 212 BC, a soldier found Archimedes in the courtyard of his house drawing diagrams in the sand. When questioned by the soldier about what he was doing, he is said to have replied: 'Go away and let me finish my work.' The soldier was so offended that he killed Archimedes on the spot despite the fact that all the Romans had been told to make sure that the famous Greek was captured alive.

Archimedes was born in Syracuse in 287 BC and, apart from some time spent studying at Alexandria in Egypt, lived there all his life. The son of a minor nobleman, who may have been related to the King, he went to Alexandria to study under a teacher called Conon and to use the resources in its great library and museum. He came under the influence of other Greeks who had worked there earlier, such as Euclid and Pythagoras, and came into contact with Eratosthenes, who was also a student. It is said that Archimedes often became so engrossed in his studies that he went for days without food and without washing.

Above all, Archimedes was a scientist who enjoyed trying out his ideas in a practical situation. His invention of a spiral screw inside a tube for lifting water from one level to another was developed when the King of Syracuse asked him to empty the hull of a ship that had filled with water. The method is still used in some African countries for getting water into irrigation ditches. He also worked with pulleys and levers and the way they could be used to lift heavy weights, studied the stars and planets and devised weapons that were tested in the defence of Syracuse when the Romans invaded. These included a giant catapult for hurling rocks, and cranes fixed to the quayside that attempted to pull Roman ships out of the water.

But the most famous story in which he features occurred when the King of Syracuse believed the new crown that had just been made for him was not 100 per cent solid gold. The King suspected his goldsmith had cheated him by adding some silver to it. Archimedes is said to have filled three containers with the same amount of water. Into one container he put a lump of gold equal to the amount of gold supposedly used in the crown. Into the second went the same weight of silver and into the third, the crown. The water level rose higher for the lump of silver than for the gold. In the container with the crown, the water rose higher than the one with the block of pure gold so Archimedes knew that the crown must be a mixture of gold and silver.

From this practical test he developed his law of hydrostatics, now called Archimedes' Principle. It states that an object placed in water loses weight equal to the weight of the water it displaces, which is why heavy metal ships float. He is said to have hit on the idea when he stepped into a bath that his servants had filled right to the brim. The water then overflowed on to the floor; but whether Archimedes raced naked down the street shouting *Eureka*!, the Greek for 'I've found it', may be just a legend.

As a mathematician, Archimedes worked with 2D and 3D shapes, looking particularly at the surface areas and volumes of cylinders, cones and spheres. Several books in which he wrote about these shapes still survive. He is also credited with establishing the relationship between the diameter and circumference of a circle that is now known by the Greek letter pi (π). Archimedes realised that it was always the same no matter what the size of the circle. He fixed it at $3\frac{1}{7}$ or $\frac{22}{7}$. In more recent times this has been converted to the decimal number 3.14.

ARCHIMEDES' PRINCIPLE

First, set the children some volume problems using the displacement process. They will need a clear plastic container, a bowl to stand it in, some water and a collection of different objects. Explain that they will be experimenting with placing different objects into a container filled with water and they will be estimating how much water will spill out. They should make a recording sheet for their estimates and actual measurements and should not be concerned if, at least initially, their estimates are inaccurate.

Then place an object in the water, collect the water that spills out and check the amount in a measuring jug. Compare with earlier estimations. Discuss how the volume of the water that overflows equals the volume of the object that displaces it. It is important to point out that 1 millilitre of water has the same volume as 1 cubic centimetre. Find the volume of irregular objects such as stones using the method shown in Figure 6.1.

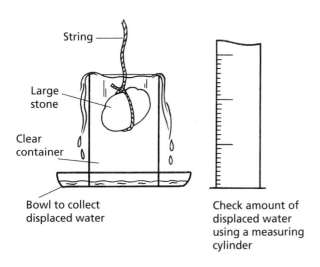

String

Large stone

Clear container

Bowl to collect displaced water

Check amount of displaced water using a measuring cylinder

● **Figure 6.1**

Also test out the children's understanding of the conservation of volume using the task outlined on the photocopiable sheet at the end of this chapter. Try a lump of plasticine or clay first. Using a wide measuring cylinder, check to see how many millilitres the water level has risen. Is the volume the same if the lump is changed into different shapes? Then use unifix or multilink cubes as shown on the worksheet. Is the volume the same if the shapes made by the cubes are altered? It is important, though, that the same numbers of cubes are used each time.

In conjunction with these activities children will need plenty of practice establishing whether quantities of liquid are less than a litre, about a litre and more than a litre. They will also need to experience taking readings from scales marked on a range of different measuring cylinders, especially those using divisions of 100 ml, 50 ml and 25 ml.

Among the tasks which small groups could work on would be:

- Use a felt-tip pen to mark levels on the side of 1-litre and 2-litre drinks bottles and then ask the children to estimate how much water would be needed to fill to this level. Use measuring jugs to check out estimates.
- Make a collection of containers and ask the children to estimate how many 5ml spoonfuls it will take to fill them up. Then use spoons to check how good the estimates were.
- Check the addition and subtraction of capacity amounts practically, for example:
  - Do the amounts 300 ml and 250 ml reach the 550 ml level when poured into an empty cylinder?
  - If 400 ml is poured out of a measuring cylinder holding half a litre, is 100 ml left?
  - How many millilitres are there in one and half litres?

In all these activities, careless spillages must be avoided if accurate results are to be produced.

As a variation from water work, investigate finding the volume of some three-dimensional shapes by filling them with sand. Take four identical pieces of thin A4 card and, using the entire card and not overlapping at the join, make them into a square prism, an equilateral triangular prism, a cylinder and a cone. Each shape should be 21 cm high. This is the width of the card. Use sticky tape all the way up the join to hold the shapes together (Figure 6.2). Estimates should now be made of the volume of each shape. Then stand them one at a time inside a measuring container and, holding the shape firmly together, pour in sand. Lift out each shape carefully when it is full and let the sand fall into the container where, when it has been shaken level, it can be measured. The cone will need to be tipped over carefully to empty its contents. Record the answers. Which held the most sand and how accurate were the estimates? Can the children explain why these results were obtained?

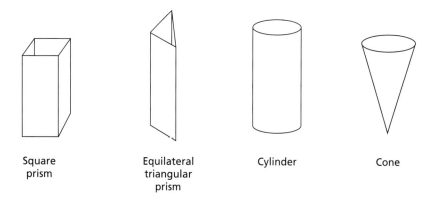

Square prism   Equilateral triangular prism   Cylinder   Cone

- **Figure 6.2:** Shapes to fill with sand

THE IMPORTANCE OF PI

The exact relationship between the diameter and circumference of a circle has puzzled mathematicians for centuries. As early as 3000 BC, the Babylonians had worked out that it was about 3. Archimedes defined it more precisely as 3¹/₇, while modern computers can calculate it to many millions of decimal places.

Ask children to collect circular objects such as hoops, wheels, tin lids and rings. Using rulers and tapes, measure their diameters accurately. Circumferences can be calculated using cotton or string, callipers or by rolling the object for one complete turn along a straight line. Compare the results collected in the table provided on the photocopiable sheet *Going round in circles*. What do the children notice? What is the ratio of the circumference to the diameter to the nearest whole number?

Metrilogs

Use the children's understanding of the term circumference to construct a metrilog – a device for measuring curved lines or distances on maps. It can prove very useful for finding the perimeter of irregular shapes such as islands or the routes followed by winding footpaths. From thick card cut the two pieces that are shown in Figure 6.3 and fix them together using a paper fastener. With a felt-tip pen, mark a straight line from the centre to the circumference (a radius). A circle with a radius of 4 cm, diameter 8 cm, will measure almost exactly 25 cm each time it does a complete turn or revolution (3.14 × 8 cm = 25.12 cm).

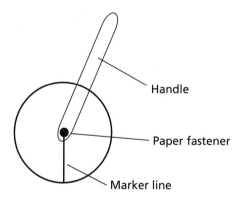

Handle

Paper fastener

Marker line

● **Figure 6.3:** A metrilog or mini trundle wheel

Finding the area of a circle

When the Ancient Egyptians wanted to find the area of a circle they drew the largest possible square they could make both inside and outside the shape. They then knew that the area of the circle lay somewhere between the areas of these two squares. Archimedes took this a stage further and closer to an accurate result by drawing polygons inside the circle instead, sometimes with as many as 96 sides. Today, mathematicians use the formula pi r squared (πr^2; r is the length of the radius of the circle) to obtain a precise answer, but there is a practical way to get close to a correct solution.

Draw a large circle on paper or thin card using a pair of compasses or drawing round a circular object. Now work out the area using the formula to see how accurate the practical result will be. Fold the circle in half and then in half again and keep folding until it has been divided into eight equal segments. Open out the circle, flatten down the folds and cut out each of the sections shown by the fold lines (Figure 6.4). This will leave a number of wedge- shaped pieces of paper. Lay the pieces down in jigsaw fashion and glue them on to paper to make as accurate a rectangle as possible (Figure 6.5). Measure and record the length and the breadth of this rectangle. Now multiply the two numbers together to find out what the area of the rectangle will be. How does it compare with the result found by using the actual formula? The difference in the results will show how important it was for mathematicians and scientists to find a precise way of finding key measurements in a circle.

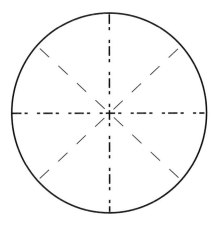

● **Figure 6.4:** Circle showing fold marks

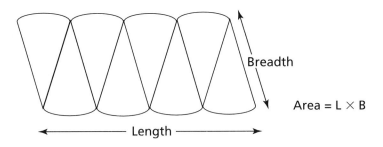

Breadth

Area = L × B

Length

● **Figure 6.5**

Unexpected results?

Conclude the circle work with an investigation that illustrates there can be occasions in maths when what appears to be a logical prediction can be shown to be incorrect. Draw large circles like the ones shown in Figure 6.6. Keep increasing the number of points marked on the circumference and join them up using straight lines. After completing two points and three points, ask the children to estimate the number of regions made by marking four points, five points and six points. Has a pattern of numbers already been established? Results should be written in a box similar to the one shown in Figure 6.7. Then draw in the lines and count the regions. Did the predictions match the actual results? Is there an explanation for what happened?

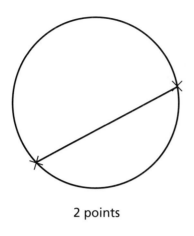
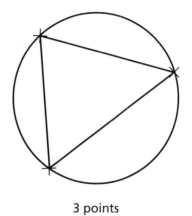

2 points   3 points

● **Figure 6.6**

Number of points on circle	2	3	4	5	6
Estimate of number of parts of circle					
Actual number of parts of circle	2	4			

● **Figure 6.7**

SUPPORT

Ensure that the scales on measuring cylinders are easy to read and that divisions are in straightforward units such as 100 ml or 50 ml. Encourage estimation, although results may be inaccurate to start with; estimating skills will improve with practice. Use mixed-ability pairs for practical work to give support. Spend time consolidating the litre as a basic unit of capacity. Assist with the construction of 3D shapes for sand work, providing nets if necessary, and help with cutting and fixing. Provide help with circle measurements, especially when finding the circumference, and use calculators to work out and/or check multiplication sums involving 3.14. In the regions task, give the children circles already drawn and with points marked on them. Check systematic counting of the regions, marking each one in turn.

EXTENSION

Encourage estimation of the volume of large objects before they are placed in the water to obtain a more exact result. Set more complex questions involving the addition and subtraction of water amounts. Use key fractions of a litre and look at different ways of writing the same measurement, for example, ¼ of a litre = 250 ml, and 1300 ml may be written as 1 l 300 ml or 1.300 l. See if the children can work out their own nets of the 3D shapes. When finding pi, widen the size of circles used, for example, from bottle top to large plastic hoop or bicycle wheel. Encourage pencil and paper calculations with decimal numbers (3.14) and use calculators to check results. During the task on regions, extend the investigation to look at seven points, eight points and beyond. What is the best method of counting? Does the pattern continue?

NATIONAL NUMERACY STRATEGY LINKS

Year 4
Main teaching activity

- Understand decimal notation and use it in context.
- Make and investigate a general statement about familiar shapes by finding examples that satisfy it.
- Use, read and write standard metric units including their abbreviations.
- Suggest suitable units and measuring equipment to estimate or measure capacity.
- Record estimates and readings from scales to a suitable degree of accuracy.
- Describe and visualise 3D and 2D shapes.
- Make shapes by paper folding.

Year 6
Main teaching activity

As Year 4 plus:

- Solve simple problems involving ratio and proportion.
- Use decimal notation for tenths and hundredths in calculations, and tenths, hundredths and thousandths when recording measurements.
- Know what each digit represents in a number with up to three decimal places.
- Develop from explaining a generalised relationship in words to expressing it in a formula using letters as symbols.
- Know the relationships between standard metric units.
- Convert smaller metric units to larger ones.
- Describe and visualise properties of solid shapes.
- Make shapes with increasing accuracy.

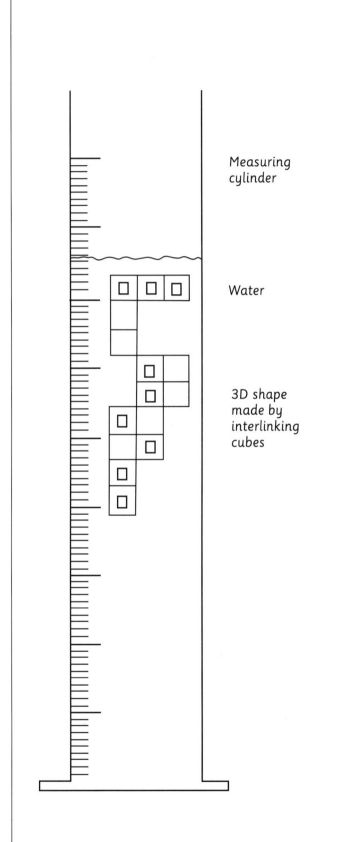

Measuring
cylinder

Water

3D shape
made by
interlinking
cubes

- Put some water into the
  measuring cylinder to the
  100 ml mark.

- Fasten 15 cubes together
  and carefully drop them into
  the water.

- Check and record how
  much the water level has
  risen.

- Take out the cubes and
  check that the water level is
  still at 100 ml.

- Make a different shape
  with the cubes and drop
  them into the water again.

- Measure how far the
  water level has risen this
  time.

- Repeat with other shapes
  made of 15 cubes. What do
  you notice?

Estimate how many mls the level
will rise if you use 20 or 30 cubes.
Check your answers.

solids as 'Euclidean geometry'. Some have even described *The Elements*, next to the Bible, as the most translated, published and studied of all the books produced in the western world. The first translation of the book into Latin was carried out by a scholar called Adelard of Bath in about 1120. He travelled around Europe disguised as a Muslim student, gathering information. By the fifteenth century printed versions were beginning to appear in Europe.

Unfortunately, we know little about Euclid as a person. He is thought to have lived about 300 BC. He was probably educated in Athens by pupils of Plato, another famous Greek scholar, but spent most of his life at Alexandria in Egypt, where he set up a school of mathematics at the request of King Ptolemy. Here he had access to the work of important mathematicians who had come before him such as Pythagoras and Eudoxus, and it was at the school set up by Euclid that Archimedes came to study later on.

In writing *The Elements*, Euclid used the skills he had acquired as a teacher to describe, explain and further develop the work of his predecessors in such a systematic way that they could be easily understood. He was an expert editor, and where he found gaps or thought that information was out of date he was able to replace it with his own theories and proofs. The skilful way in which he did this acted later as a model for the development of other branches of mathematics.

Despite this patient approach, there is evidence to suggest that he had little time for those who were not prepared to take his work seriously or to spend time and effort in study and research. When King Ptolemy asked him once if there was quick way to find solutions to the type of mathematical problems found in *The Elements*, Euclid is said to have replied: 'I am afraid there is no royal road to geometry.' On another occasion when he heard a student complaining about what he actually got out of learning subjects such as geometry, the great teacher turned to a servant and said: 'Give him some coins since he must needs make gain by what he learns.'

It would be wrong to think of Euclid as just a theoretical mathematician. He tried to show in many ways how his findings could be applied to science and engineering. He investigated why some shapes, especially triangles, are rigid, while others, such as squares and rectangles, do not have the same qualities of strength. Many of today's large structures, including high-rise buildings and bridges, are built on the principles which he discussed. He was also one of the first mathematicians to examine the importance of parallel lines and, in another of his books, called *Optics*, linked his theories on these special types of lines to the way in which rays of light travel from the sun.

His name obviously still meant a great deal to a group of American surveyors and architects who mapped out the land and planned a new city on the shores of Lake Erie in Ohio during the year 1798. The real reason is not certain, but they called the city Euclid, in honour of the great mathematician. It is now a manufacturing centre with a range of different industries and has a population of over 50,000.

MAKING 3D SHAPES

Provide the children with some background information about Euclid and let them start their own investigations of his work by finding out how to make one of the most common 3D shapes: the cube. On the photocopiable sheet at the end of this chapter, several successful nets are provided. Ask the children to test out some of the others that are shown and then try to find all the possible solutions. All these shapes are called hexominoes because they have an area of six squares. There should be a total of eleven correct nets altogether. Remember that all the nets will need to have flaps added for gluing if they are to be fixed permanently.

Suggest that they also make the same shape but this time by plaiting; 2 cm or larger squared paper is best. Using the diagram shown in Figure 7.1, cut along the solid line as far as the point marked X. All the dotted lines should be folded over. Begin plaiting by putting a on top of b, and then make up the four faces of the cube by folding c around the base of a and b. Wrap over a and b to complete the shape, and tuck in the flap to hold it together.

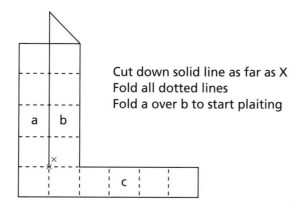

Cut down solid line as far as X
Fold all dotted lines
Fold a over b to start plaiting

● **Figure 7.1**

Challenge the children to devise a net for making a cuboid by the same process. Spend some time first examining a range of different cuboid boxes especially those commonly used for packaging. It is worthwhile taking some examples apart carefully and then reconstructing them to show how the net makes up into the finished article. Plaiting the cuboid is a difficult task and most children will need help and advice. To construct one from a cube that has already been made, these two rules may prove to be helpful:

1   Write on the cube which faces need to become rectangles.
2   As the cube is unplaited, each time a face with the word rectangle on it is lifted, the same word should also be written on the face that has become uncovered.

Once these solids have been constructed, time should be taken to make sure that the children are aware of their properties. Discuss in what ways the two shapes are similar and in what ways they are different. Focus on key vocabulary that will also be needed when more complex 3D shapes are featured later. Check on their understanding of words such as face, edge and vertex (corner) and that they can use a systematic approach to counting how many of each of these they have. Remind them that edges are where two faces meet and corners are where a number of edges meet.

When the children have become more skilled at making 3D shapes, try this challenge as a small group activity. Ask each group to make six small cuboids (66 mm × 33 mm), three 33 mm cubes and an open-topped 100 mm cube. Is it possible to pack all the small shapes into the large cube successfully?

If the children are familiar with cube-shaped dice, set them this problem-solving task. The nets of the cubes shown in Figure 7.2 have numbers missing from them. Can they fill in the empty squares with the correct digits, bearing in mind that only 1–6 can be used, that no numbers should be repeated and that the opposite faces of the cube must add up to seven. Those with good spatial awareness may be able to fill in the numbers and then check out their answers by putting the cube together. Others may need to carry out the construction first.

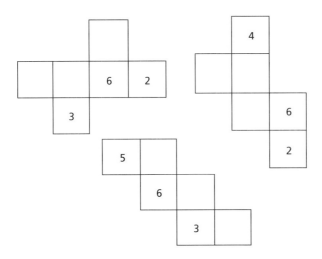

● **Figure 7.2**

Move on to investigate nets that will make up other 3D shapes. Use dotty or isometric paper, for example, to find how many different nets there are for making the tetrahedron or triangular-based pyramid. One is shown in Figure 7.3.

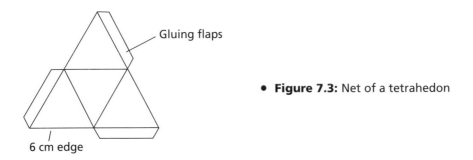

● **Figure 7.3:** Net of a tetrahedon

Although two different nets are needed, it is possible to make five tetrahedrons that will fit inside an open cube. Four can made using the net that has been provided already, while the remaining one is made up from the net shown in Figure 7.4. This consists of a large equilateral triangle in the centre surrounded by three half squares.

Use this net to make the cube (Figure 7.5). The edge length of the squares that make up the net of this cube should be just a little longer than the shorter edge length of the half squares mentioned above to make sure they fit inside comfortably.

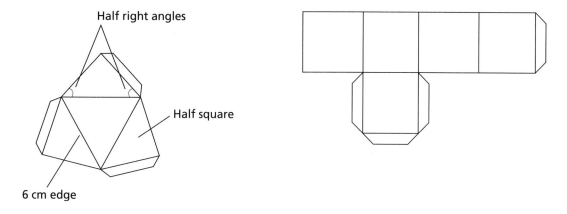

Half right angles

Half square

6 cm edge

- **Figure 7.4:** Another net of a tetrahedron   - **Figure 7.5:** Net of open cube

It should be pointed out to the children that although the cube has more faces than the tetrahedron and is made from squares and not triangles, the two shapes do have something in common. They belong to a group of shapes called the Five Platonic Polyhedra. They take their name from the Greek philosopher Plato and are linked because all their faces are regular, that is, the same shape and size. In addition to the cube and tetrahedron, the other members of the family are the octahedron, made from eight triangles and having eight identical faces, the icosahedron, with twenty triangular faces, and the dodecahedron with twelve faces in the shape of a regular pentagon. The nets for these other three shapes are given in Figure 7.6.

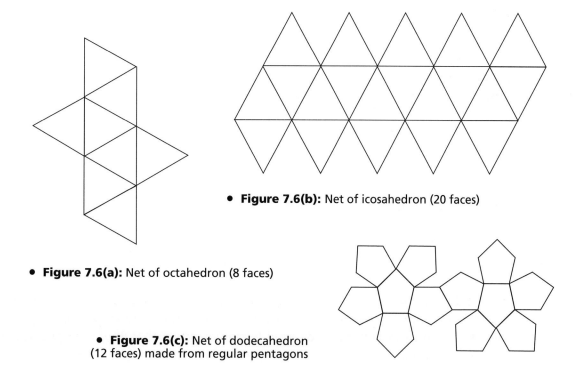

- **Figure 7.6(b):** Net of icosahedron (20 faces)

- **Figure 7.6(a):** Net of octahedron (8 faces)

- **Figure 7.6(c):** Net of dodecahedron (12 faces) made from regular pentagons

Activities involving the tetrahedron or triangular-based pyramid will highlight its differences from the pyramid the children may be more familiar with – the Egyptian or square-based version. Two possible nets for this shape are provided on the photocopiable sheet *The Egyptian pyramid*, but the gluing flaps have been omitted and children should find out how many are required and where they should be positioned. Once the shape has been constructed, discuss its properties:

- How many faces are there and what shape are they?
- How many edges are there?
- How many corners does it have?

Using construction straws or art straws held together by sticky tape, ask the children to construct a range of skeletal 3D shapes including ones which have already been discussed, such as the cube, cuboid and two types of pyramid. Some examples of these are shown in Figure 7.7. This is a particularly good method for those who have difficulty calculating the number of edges and corners in each of the shapes as edges have to be measured and cut before construction and corners become automatic fixing points.

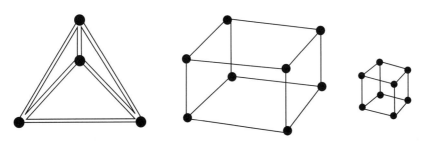

- **Figure 7.7:** Skeletal shapes

Building with strong triangles

Extend this task by investigating how much stronger are 3D shapes based on triangles compared with those made from other polygons. Find pictures of bridges, towers and other structures, especially those made from metal where the girder work is clearly visible. The Forth Bridge, the Eiffel Tower, electricity pylons, the configuration of rafters that go to make up the roof of a house, and five-barred gates are good examples. Discuss what shapes are being used in them and how they help to give the structure its strength.

Simple tests on rigidity and strength can be carried out using lengths of thick card connected with paper fasteners or strips made of plastic or metal such as Meccano. Make up some shapes with four sides (quadrilaterals) and five sides (pentagons) and see how many diagonal pieces need to be added to the structure to make it rigid (Figure 7.8). Try shapes with six, seven and eight sides. Set the results down in a table and see if there is a pattern to the answers (Figure 7.9). An experiment like this will help children to understand that the triangle is the only rigid polygon and that other polygons can only be made rigid by adding struts that divide the shape up into a series of triangles.

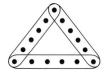
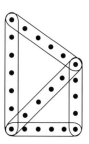
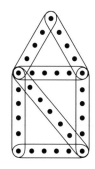

Number of sides in polygon	Number of diagnols to make it rigid
3	0
4	1
5	2
6	
7	
8	

● **Figure 7.9:** Making shapes rigid

● **Figure 7.8**

Parallel lines

Parallel lines are lines that stay the same distance apart all the way along their length, as opposed to divergent lines, which move further apart, and convergent lines, which gradually meet. Just a quick look around the classroom and at other school buildings will reveal the importance of parallel lines in construction. Look for brick courses, the frameworks of windows and doors, and where walls and ceilings join.

Use strips of card and paper fasteners to show how shapes such as the square and the rectangle can be converted into a rhombus and a parallelogram by pushing them over to one side. Here the shape changes but the sides still remain parallel (Figure 7.10). Make sets of parallel lines on geoboards with elastic bands and use them for building 2D shapes. Start with squares and rectangles but move on to rhombus, parallelogram and trapezium (Figure 7.11).

 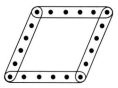

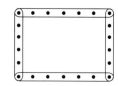

● **Figure 7.10(a):** Square deformed to make rhombus

● **Figure 7.10(b):** Rectangle deformed to make parallelogram

This net will fold to make a cube.

Here are some more nets. Which ones will make cubes?

Try to find all the possible nets of a cube:

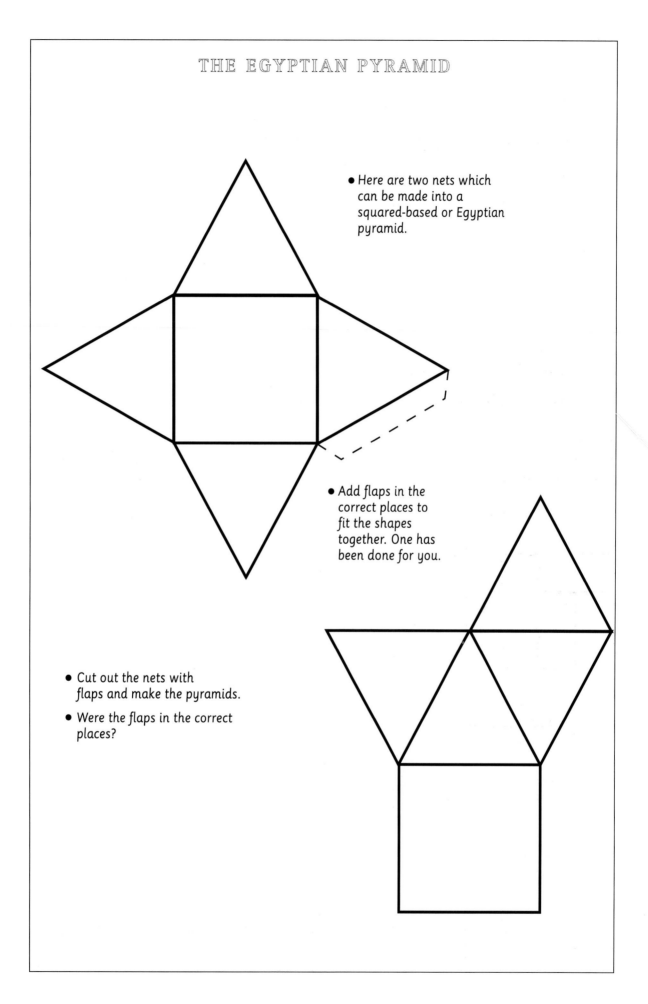

● Here are two nets which can be made into a squared-based or Egyptian pyramid.

● Add flaps in the correct places to fit the shapes together. One has been done for you.

● Cut out the nets with flaps and make the pyramids.

● Were the flaps in the correct places?

8
Pythagoras
Studying in quietness and solitude

The teachings of the Greek scientist and mathematician Pythagoras became so unpopular at certain points in his lifetime that on two occasions he and his followers had to move to escape persecution.

Pythagoras was born about 580 BC on the small Ionian island of Samos in the Aegean Sea. As a youngster he studied under the famous philosopher Thales. At that time each part of Greece had its own ruler and for many years Pythagoras got on well with the King of Samos, Polycrates, who encouraged poets, artists, scientists and craftsmen. But when the King became cruel and tyrannical Pythagoras knew it was time to leave. His journey took him to Crotona, a Greek colony in southern Italy. Here he and his followers lived peacefully for many years, but later there were problems with the local people, and after several buildings were burnt down in an attack they finally settled in Metapontum, where Pythagoras died in 500 BC.

On each occasion that Pythagoras moved he took with him a group of some 300 people who, because of their close attachment to him, became known as the Pythagoreans. The community studied religion, politics and philosophy as well as science and maths. There were strict rules of obedience for the members of the community and they were often required to spend long periods of time in silence. They were only allowed to eat certain foods, they wore simple clothes and kept very few possessions. Most of their time was spent studying and thinking. Many believed in reincarnation – people's souls being reborn in another body. Pythagoras, for example, thought that in a previous life he had been, among other things, a soldier in the Trojan War. He had been permitted to bring into this life the memory of his former existences.

In all their studies the followers of Pythagoreanism believed that numbers controlled everything in life. This applied not only to maths but also to science, astronomy, art, architecture and music. Nature was based on number ratios and proportion and it was number that gave the universe its order and harmony.

Among the mathematical investigations that they carried out were studies into odd and even numbers, primes, square numbers and proportion. In geometry, the chief discovery of the group was what is now called Pythagoras' Theorem. The great man himself never wrote or published a book and it was only through the writings of his disciples later that this rule about the properties of right-angled triangles became widely known. They also established that the sum of the internal angles in a triangle was equal to two right angles and that some shapes, including equilateral triangles, fitted together without leaving gaps between them. This process is now called tessellation, from the Latin word *tesserae*, meaning a small tile or piece of mosaic.

As astronomers, Pythagoras and his followers were the first to consider the earth as a sphere that was revolving with others planets around a central fire. In music they carried out detailed research into how notes were played. They examined the musical instruments of the time such as the lyre and came to the conclusion that the sound produced depended on the mathematical relationship between the length of the vibrating string and how tightly it was stretched. The closer a string was pressed, the shorter the part that vibrated and the higher the note that was made. They linked their ideas on astronomy and music by saying that because the planets were separated from each other like the notes made on an instrument, they gave rise to a musical sound which they called the harmony of the spheres.

TESTING OUT THE THEOREM

Pythagoras' Theorem states that in every right-angled triangle the squares on the two shorter sides are equal to the square on the third and longest side. This is called the hypotenuse. The theorem can easily be to tested out practically using squared paper, and details are given on the photocopiable sheet at the end of this chapter. Try other methods, such as using string or stretching elastic bands on a geoboard. Larger versions can also be made outside on the school field or playground. Join some ropes together and mark off twelve units of equal length. Then shape the rope into the triangle shown in Figure 8.1 and a right angle should be produced. Variations of this method were used by the Ancient Egyptians when they were pyramid building because they were then guaranteed that the square base of the shape would always have good right angles. Ask the children to check out if a right angle is produced when the sides of the 3, 4, 5 triangle are increased in equal proportion. Does it still work, for example, if the units are doubled to give 6, 8, 10 or trebled to make 9, 12, 15?

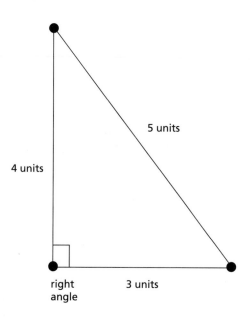

5 units

4 units

right angle

3 units

● **Figure 8.1:** Rope stretching

This process can be taken a stage further to investigate the pattern of numbers that is often called Pythagorean triads or triples. These are sets of whole numbers which demonstrate that if the sides of any triangle fit the pattern $a^2 + b^2 = c^2$ then it must have a right angle. Some examples of these triples have been given in the table shown in Figure 8.2. Ask the children to provide others and also to look for the pattern made by the numbers as they progress. There are significant features to be found in all three columns.

Side A	Side B	Side C
3	4	5
5	12	13
7	24	25
9	40	41

● **Figure 8.2:** Triads pattern

The properties of triangles

A simple practical task can also be carried out to show children that the internal angles of a triangle always total two right angles or 180 degrees. Establish first that the children understand that the angle about a straight line is made up of two 90 degree angles so has to be 180 degrees (Figure 8.3). Ask them to cut out a selection of large triangles from card or coloured sugar paper. Number the angles in each triangle 1, 2 and 3. In each case the three angles of the triangle should be ripped off carefully and then arranged so that the numbered corners of the triangle lie along a straight line. The children should then be able to see that, because they make a straight line, they must total 180 degrees (Figure 8.4).

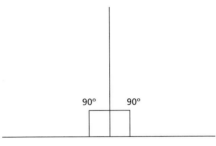

The angle about a straight line = 90° + 90° = 180°

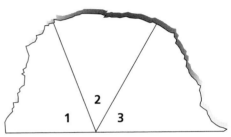

The three angles torn form a straight line so internal angles of a triangle = 180°

● **Figure 8.3**

● **Figure 8.4**

Use the same method to help children discover that the internal angles of any quadrilateral are equal to four right angles or 360 degrees. Demonstrate, by using Figure 8.5, that a vertical and a horizontal line can cross each other to form four right angles or a complete turn of 360 degrees. A variety of different four-sided shapes should then be cut out and the four angles in each corner numbered before being torn off carefully. The complete turn of 360 degrees can then be made if the angles are rearranged as shown in Figure 8.6.

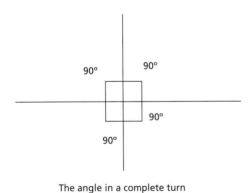

The angle in a complete turn
equals 90° + 90° + 90° + 90° = 360°

● **Figure 8.5**

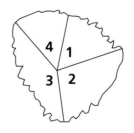

Four angles from a quadrilateral make a complete turn so must equal 360°

● **Figure 8.6**

Families of triangles

At this point discuss with the children the range of different triangles which can be made and how they can be grouped into families. Triangles can either be drawn on dotty paper or constructed using elastic bands on geoboards. Set particular targets to get a wide range of shapes; ask, for example: How many different triangles can you make with only one dot (or pin) inside them?

Explain that triangles can be classified by a number of different factors. These include the length of their sides, their angles and how many lines of reflective symmetry they have. Triangles with three equal sides are called equilateral triangles. Those with two equal sides, isosceles, and those with three different sides, scalene. Triangles can also be right-angled (with an angle of 90 degrees), acute-angled (with angles less than 90 degrees) and obtuse-angled (with one angle more than 90 degrees). They can have no lines of symmetry, one line of symmetry or three lines of symmetry. Venn diagrams or Carroll diagrams are useful for showing the similarities and differences in a collection of triangles. Check on properties by asking such questions as:

- How many right angles can a triangle ever have?
- How big is each of the acute angles in an equilateral triangle?
- Are triangles with one or more lines of symmetry always isosceles?
- Is it possible to have a triangle with two lines of symmetry?
- Do triangles with three lines of symmetry have to be equilateral?

Use mirrors to check out whether triangles are symmetrical or not.

Finding the area of a triangle

Introduce finding the area of triangles with this activity. On isometric paper, draw the sequence of triangles illustrated in Figure 8.7. Record in a table the number of units making up one side of the triangle and its area. An identifiable pattern should soon begin to emerge. Then encourage the children to think in terms of the area of a triangle being half that of the area of the square or rectangle which encloses it. In Figure 8.8, for example, the area of the triangle will be half of the area of the square, that is, half of 4 cm × 4 cm, which is 8 cm². Figure 8.9 shows that if the area of the rectangle is 24 cm², the area of the triangle must be half that amount, which is 12 cm². This will provide a good basis later for establishing that the area of any triangle will be half the product of the base and the height.

Side = 1 unit   Side = 2 unit   Side = 3 unit
Area = 1 unit   Area = 4 unit   Area = 9 unit

- **Figure 8.7**

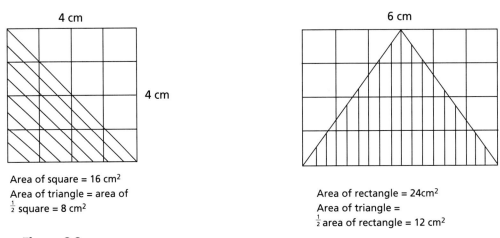

Area of square = 16 cm²
Area of triangle = area of
$\frac{1}{2}$ square = 8 cm²

● **Figure 8.8**

Area of rectangle = 24cm²
Area of triangle =
$\frac{1}{2}$ area of rectangle = 12 cm²

● **Figure 8.9**

For those who are able to move on, try this investigation which examines the area of growing right-angled isosceles triangles. Ask the children to draw the three triangles on squared paper as shown in Figure 8.10. Can they find the area of the triangles in square units? Remember that they will need a strategy for dealing with half squares. From what they have discovered they should be able to predict what the area of larger triangles in the sequence will be. Drawing the triangles will enable them to check out their solutions. Finally, look at the differences between the answers as the triangles grow in size to see what pattern has been formed.

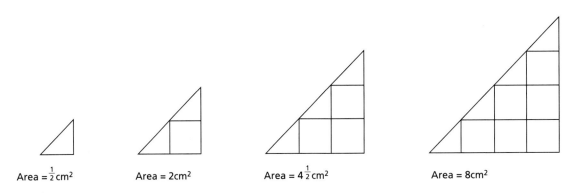

Area = $\frac{1}{2}$ cm²   Area = 2cm²   Area = $4\frac{1}{2}$ cm²   Area = 8cm²

● **Figure 8.10:** Growing triangles

Tessellation

Start tessellation tasks with equilateral triangles. As well as the many attractive patterns that can be made with them as art and maths integrates, try to introduce some structure into the sessions. Investigate how many different shapes can be made with two of these triangles, then try three, four and five. Or start with the six equilateral triangles that can be made by cutting up a regular hexagon (see the photocopiable sheet, *Tessellating triangles*). This time, name specific shapes that the children have to make. Ask them, for example, to make a large triangle from four smaller ones. Can they join two pieces together to make a rhombus? How would they make a parallelogram in a four-piece tessellation? Can they show a trapezium with three of the triangles? How would they construct an irregular pentagon with five?

Fun with triangles

Round off the work on triangles with some problem-solving tasks using coins and matchsticks that have had their heads removed:

- Figure 8.11 shows an arrangement of three triangles made with matches. Is it possible to make five triangles by moving only three of the matches?
- In Figure 8.12 six identical rectangles have been made using a total of thirteen matches. The task this time is to remove one of the matches yet still be able to make six shapes which are exactly the same size. Clue: Think about the hexagon from a previous activity.
- Set up a triangle made from small coins or counters (Figure 8.13). What is the smallest numbers of coins or counters that need to be moved to change the pattern into a triangle that is pointing down? Or take three 2p coins and three 1p coins and arrange them to form a triangle so that each of its sides add up to 5p.
- Now try this one. A family has a pond in their garden. The shape of the pond is an equilateral triangle and three trees have been planted at the corners of the triangle (see Figure 8.14). How can they enlarge the pond so that it is four times as large and still an equilateral triangular shape? Moving the trees is not allowed and of course the trees must not be in the water or on islands.

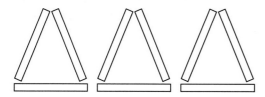

Make 5 triangles by moving only three matches.

- **Figure 8.11**

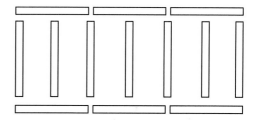

Use 12 matchsticks to make 6 shapes which are exactly the same.

- **Figure 8.12**

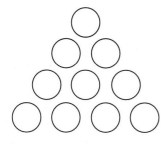

- **Figure 8.13**

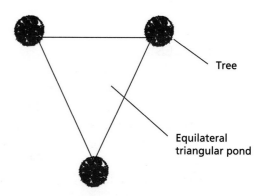

Tree

Equilateral triangular pond

- **Figure 8.14**

SUPPORT

Children may find it easier when working on Pythagoras' Theorem if they use larger squared paper, for example, 2 cm squares. If they are trying out the 3, 4, 5 rope-stretching activity, provide ropes which have already been marked with the 12 units. Permit the use of a calculator for speed and accuracy when the children are working on Pythagorean triples. Assist with the drawing of large triangles to find angles. Also help with tearing off and arranging the angles to make a straight line. The work on the area of a triangle should start with simple tasks where small triangles are counted up inside larger ones. Allow plenty of experimentation to take place on large isometric paper when investigating the ways in which triangles tessellate. Pair up children to work on puzzle questions, encouraging the use of a 'hands on' approach.

EXTENSION

Encourage as much prediction as possible when Pythagorean triads are being calculated and let children use their own written methods of multiplication. Ask them to produce a range of different triangles when they are working on the sum of the angles of a triangle being 180 degrees to show that the same solution will be reached no matter what the type or size of triangle. Provide opportunities for the children to become proficient with angle measurers. They should also be able to calculate the third angle of a triangle if two angles are known. Children should show the differences and similarities between triangle families by using Venn and Carroll diagrams. Set tasks in which children have to find the area of triangles by using the formula: half the product of the base and the height. See if children can produce their own problem-solving activities with triangles using matches and/or coins.

KEY VOCABULARY

Hypotenuse, theorem, pattern, puzzle, calculate, calculation, Carroll diagram, Venn diagram, angle, triangle, triangular, equilateral triangle, isosceles triangle, scalene triangle, right angle, acute angle, obtuse angle, degree, straight line, revolution, quadrilateral, rhombus, parallelogram, trapezium, regular, irregular, pentagon, hexagon, pyramid, line of symmetry, mirror line, reflective symmetry, same, similar, different.

RESOURCES

Squared paper (1 cm and 2 cm), isometric paper ($\frac{1}{2}$ cm and $2\frac{1}{2}$ cm), dotty paper, coloured sugar paper or thin card, scissors, sticky tape, glue, geoboards, elastic bands, calculators, matchsticks (heads removed), coins or coloured counters, photocopiable pages 92 and 93.

NATIONAL NUMERACY STRATEGY LINKS

Year 4
Main teaching activity

- Solve mathematical problems or puzzles, recognise and explain patterns and relationships, generalise and predict.
- Make and investigate a general statement about familiar shapes.
- Solve a problem by collecting quickly, organising, representing and interpreting data in tables, for example, Venn and Carroll diagrams.
- Recognise equilateral and isosceles triangles.
- Make shapes, for example, using a pinboard and discuss properties such as lines of symmetry.

Year 6
Main teaching activity

As for Year 4 plus:

- Develop from explaining a generalised relationship in words to expressing it in a formula using letters as symbols; for example, finding the area of a triangle using $\frac{1}{2}$ base × height.
- Recognise and estimate angles.
- Use a protractor to measure and draw acute and obtuse angles to the nearest degree.
- Check that the sum of the angles of a triangle is 180 degrees.
- Calculate the angles in a triangle.

RIGHT-ANGLED TRIANGLES

The Greek mathematician Pythagoras found out that in any right-angled triangle, the squares on two sides totalled the square on the third side.

- Use squared paper to make this diagram:

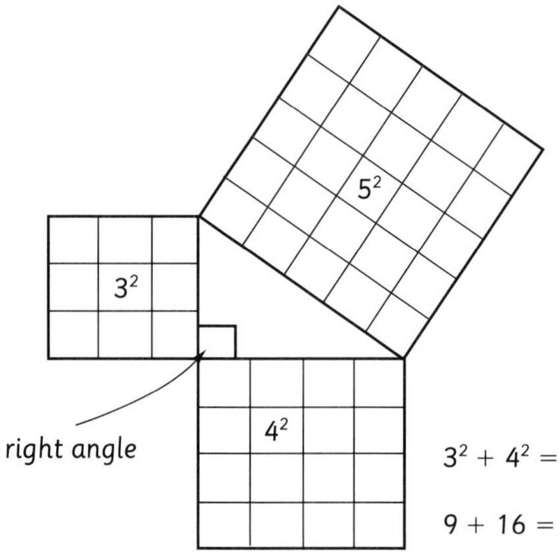

$3^2 + 4^2 = 52$

$9 + 16 = 25$

- Try this method with the sides of other triangles to see if they have a right angle in them. Draw one in the space below:

- Double the size of the 3, 4, 5 triangle. Is it still right-angled?

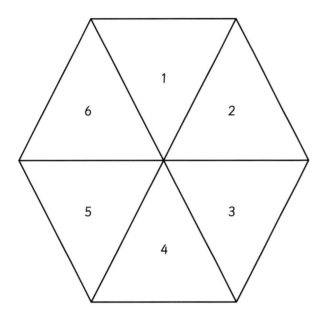

● Draw a large hexagon on isometric paper like the one shown. Divide it up into six equilateral triangles and cut them out. Use them, like pieces in a jigsaw, to solve the problems given below.

1 Can you make a large equilateral triangle using four small triangles?

2 Can you make a rhombus using two of the triangles?

3 Can you make two parallelograms, one with four triangles and one with all six triangles?

4 Can you make a trapezium with three triangles?

5 Can you make a irregular pentagon with five triangles?

6 Can you make a regular hexagon with four triangles?

7 Can you make a regular heptagon with five triangles?

8 Remake the original hexagon and look at its special properties.

other subjects including physics, astronomy, mechanics, optics and acoustics. Some of his maths publications became standard textbooks that were used by students for over one hundred years.

Born in the city of Basle in 1707, Euler studied at the local university under a famous mathematician called Jean Bernoulli, even though his father had originally intended him to become a clergyman. He graduated with a master's degree at the age of only 16 – the time now when most children are taking their GCSE examinations.

When he was 20, Euler was invited by Catherine I, Empress of Russia, to join the staff of the Academy of Sciences that she had just set up in St Petersburg. He became professor of physics in 1731 and professor of mathematics in 1733. Five years later he began to suffer problems with his vision and lost the sight in one eye because of a disease known as cataracts which causes a clouding of the lens. In 1741 he was persuaded by the King of Prussia, Frederick the Great, to join the Berlin Academy of Sciences as professor of mathematics. Here he worked closely with Bernoulli's two sons, Daniel and Nicholas. Euler stayed in this position until 1766, when he returned St Petersburg; he remained there until his death in 1783. By the time of his return to Russia the disease had spread to his other eye and the last years of his life were spent in total blindness. In recognition of his work, he was awarded a pension by the Academy in St Petersburg and continued to study and dictate information to his assistants right up until the time he died.

Euler has been described as the greatest mathematician of the eighteenth century. He was certainly responsible for setting up a system of maths education in Russia where none had existed before. He also did pioneering work in the field of algebra – the branch of mathematics where unknown amounts are represented by letters. He introduced the use of the letters a, b, and c for the three sides of a triangle and the use of the Greek letter pi (π) to describe the relationship between the diameter and circumference of a circle. His work in geometry updated many of the discoveries made in Ancient Greece by scholars such as Pythagoras and Euclid. Euler established, for example, a common relationship between the numbers of vertices, faces and edges in three-dimensional shapes. Many of his logic problems concerned the drawing of networks, a system of routes that can be followed without having to travel over the same ground twice.

But he was not just interested in the theory of mathematics. He was also keen that mathematical knowledge should be used to solve problems practically. So his ideas were put to the test in technology projects including the construction of buildings, the flow of liquids and fluids, the speed of vehicles and the control of ships. His main study in astronomy looked at the movement of the Sun, Earth and Moon and led to the making of a series of tables by the Admiralty in England that enabled sailors to find their position at sea more easily.

FINDING THE MISSING LETTER

From a young age, children will have been familiar with arithmetical problems in which they have to find a missing number. The unknown quantity will usually have been indicated by using a box, a line or a question mark as in simple problems such as $5 + \square = 12$, $\_ - 3 = 7$ and $5 \times ? = 20$. When the children are older, introduce the use of letters for missing amounts and use algebra as a way of improving understanding of important mathematical rules such as the commutative and associative laws. These laws do not necessarily have to be named as long as children understand the principles on which they work.

The commutative law

The commutative law concerns the fact that, in both addition and multiplication questions, the order in which numbers are processed has no effect on the answer. If $9 + 6 = 15$ then $6 + 9$ will produce the same solution. The same rule applies to a series of numbers, for example, if $3 + 5 + 7 = 15$, $7 + 5 + 3$ will give the same answer and so will $3 + 7 + 5$. Gradually introduce larger numbers in the questions that are given to the children and vary the position of the missing amount. Here are some examples:

- If $35 + 22 = 57$ find a in this number statement or sentence: $22 + a = 57$.
- If $27 + 34 + 39 = 100$, find the missing number shown by a in $34 + 27 + a = 100$.

  Illustrate how the rule also applies to multiplication. For example: $3 \times 5 = 15$ and $5 \times 3 = 15$. Groups of numbers being multiplied are no exception as $3 \times 4 \times 2 = 24$ and $4 \times 2 \times 3 = 24$. Again, use this knowledge to investigate missing numbers with questions such as these:

- If $7 \times 6 = 42$ complete this statement: $6 \times a = 42$.
- If $3 \times 4 \times 5 = 60$ what is the missing number in $4 \times 3 \times a = 60$?

  It will be important, however, to stress to the children that this rule does not work for subtraction and division. Discuss statements to show this. For example, $7 - 3$ does not equal $3 - 7$ and $36 \div 9$ does not produce the same answer as $9 \div 36$.

The associative law

The associative law involves the way in which numbers can be regrouped in order to make them easier to add. $12 + 23 + 18$ can be added as $12 + (23 + 18) = 53$, as $(12 + 23) + 18 = 53$ or as $(12 + 18) + 23 = 53$. Some children may find the last method simpler as it produces the round number 30 at the start.

Try the same kind of activity with multiplication. Faced with $5 \times 4 \times 3$ some children may find it easier to work out the answer using $(5 \times 4) \times 3 = 60$ while others will prefer to think in terms of $5 \times (4 \times 3) = 60$. Again set questions based on this information with letters being used for missing numbers, for example, $74 + (a + 29) = 139$ and $a \times (5 \times 3) = 75$. Remind the children that this law, like the previous one, cannot be applied to subtraction and division.

Inverse operations

While working with numbers in this way, also remind the children that both addition and subtraction and multiplication and division are inverse operations. This is particularly useful when checking the solutions to questions that have already been calculated. For example, if children have worked out that 73 + 29 = 102, they should be able to complete these statements:

- 29 + a = 102;
- 102 − a = 73;
- a − 73 = 29.

Starting from the subtraction statement 93 − 27 = 66 they should be able to work out the missing numbers in:

- 93 − a = 27;
- 66 + a = 93;
- a + 66 = 93.

Similarly, if they know that 24 x 13 = 312, ask them to solve:

- 13 × 24 = a;
- 312 ÷ a = 24;
- 312 ÷ a = 13.

Then work the other way. If 608 ÷ 32 = 19 ask them to provide the solutions for:

- 608 ÷ a = 32;
- 19 × a = 608;
- 32 × a = 608.

Round off the work on algebra with more open-ended problem-solving tasks in which questions are composed entirely of missing numbers or letters and several trial and error methods will need to be used to find successful answers. In Figure 9.1 one of the digits 1, 2, 3, 4 and 5 should be placed in each box to make the largest possible answer. The reverse should be done in Figure 9.2. This time arrange the same digits in a different order to make the smallest possible solution. Remind the children to look carefully at the operation signs. Go on to find the answers in Figure 9.3, where the letters in each question always represent a single-digit number.

- **Figure 9.1**

- **Figure 9.2**

```
        L                      A  T

          M                    A  T
    +                     
        L  M                   A  T
      ─────              +
        M  L                   A  T
      ─────                  ─────
                               P  A
    Find L and M             ─────
```

Find the letters A, T and P

● **Figure 9.3**

Euler's rule for 3D shapes

When Euler studied the numbers of vertices (corners), edges and faces in 3D shapes he discovered an important relationship. To carry out this investigation children will need at least five solid shapes that have straight rather than curved surfaces. The cube, cuboid, triangular prism, tetrahedron and squared-based pyramid make a good combination, but it should also work with other shapes. Once the shapes are gathered together, ask the children to check out this theory: Does the number of edges in these shapes always equal the number of faces added to the number of vertices, take away 2? As a formula this would be written as Edges = Faces + Vertices − 2. A box for recording and calculating the results is given in Figure 9.4. Does this version of the formula: Faces + Vertices = Edges + 2, also work?

Shape	Number of vertices	Number of faces	Vertices + faces	Number of edges

● **Figure 9.4**

Networks

In mathematics, a network is a series of intersecting lines that join up a number of points or junctions. When networks are being drawn certain important rules have to be followed:

LEONHARD EULER **99**

1   Lines must be drawn continuously without removing the pencil from the paper.
2   It is not possible to draw over a line that has already been drawn.
3   It is possible to pass through a junction more than once.

Figure 9.5 shows some examples of odd and even junctions and Figure 9.6 shows one way of successfully linking the points A, B and C using a network diagram. Arrows have been used to illustrate the direction of movement. In Figure 9.7 some other networks are shown. Ask the children if they can be drawn successfully following the instructions. Can they also formulate a rule that can be applied to all networks stating whether they can be drawn successfully or not? They should look especially at the number of odd junctions the network has. Challenge children to draw their own network diagrams. Different coloured pencils are desirable to show junctions and routes and lines should be given arrows to indicate a correct solution.

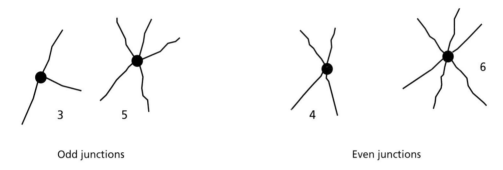

Odd junctions   Even junctions

• **Figure 9.5**

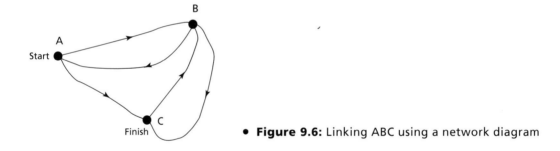

• **Figure 9.6:** Linking ABC using a network diagram

Can these networks be drawn according to the rules?

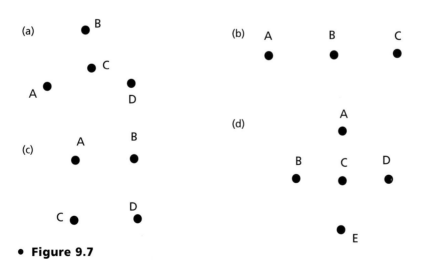

• **Figure 9.7**

The Bridges of Königsberg

Euler first became involved in the problem of networks when he studied the famous riddle of the bridges of Königsberg (see the photocopiable sheet at the end of this chapter). The German town of Königsberg was built on two islands and the banks of the River Pregel. The banks and the islands were linked by seven bridges, and for many years the citizens of the town had tried to find a route that would start at one point, cross every bridge once and return them to the same location. Euler did not need to visit Königsberg. Instead, he drew a network map from which he was able to work out a solution (Figure 9.8). He found that such a route was impossible because the network had four odd junctions. Further investigations showed Euler that a network can only be completed successfully if all the junctions are even or if only two of the junctions are odd. Any number higher than this means it is not possible. The people of Königsberg could have solved their problem either by blowing up the bridge that linked the two islands or by building a second bridge between them. Whether Euler suggested this to them or, if he did, whether they accepted his advice is not recorded.

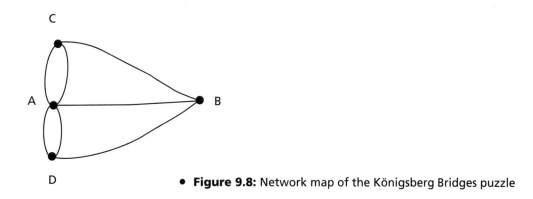

• **Figure 9.8:** Network map of the Königsberg Bridges puzzle

Being logical

Extend the children's powers of logical thinking by looking at other investigations. Both the Mobius Band and the Towers of Hanoi will provide them with the opportunity for more practical activity.

For the Mobius Band, first developed by a German mathematician during the eighteenth century, follow the making instructions that are given in Figure 9.9. Once the band is constructed, draw a line on the surface of the band. Start at the join and go round until the beginning is reached. Ask the children what they notice. Colour in one surface of the band and again ask for their observations.

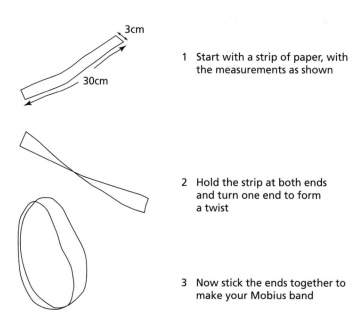

1 Start with a strip of paper, with the measurements as shown

2 Hold the strip at both ends and turn one end to form a twist

3 Now stick the ends together to make your Mobius band

• **Figure 9.9:** Making a Moibus band

If they make a cut in the middle of the band and cut all the way around, what happens?

The Towers of Hanoi puzzle comes in several different forms. It was invented by the Frenchman Edouard Lucas and first produced as a toy late in the nineteenth century. One version, which the children can easily make themselves, is given on the photocopiable sheet at the end of the chapter.

SUPPORT

In algebra work, revise statements using boxes and question marks first before moving on to the use of letters. Start commutative and associative law tasks with single-digit numbers until children understand the principle then proceed to using two-digit numbers. Provide number lines and table squares when children are working on multiplication and division, especially when looking at inverse operations. Check on and assist with systematic methods for counting the vertices, edges and faces of 3D shapes. Prepare for work on networks by revising activities such as mazes where simple routes have to be followed. Pair up children when investigating logic puzzles as two heads are often better than one.

EXTENSION

Vary the position of the missing letter in algebra questions so children have to use different strategies to find it. Move up to three-digit numbers when looking at the commutative and associative laws. Children can use digit cards and/or dice to generate their own numbers. Encourage the use of inverse operations to check calculations frequently. Provide children with three numbers and ask them to find multiplication and division statements, for example, from 8, 24, and 3 they should be able to make $3 \times 8 = 24$, $8 \times 3 = 24$, $24 \div 8 = 3$ and $24 \div 3 = 8$. Can they apply Euler's rule to other 3D shapes such as the pentagonal prism and octahedron, trying to find nets for these shapes themselves? Ask them to provide their own rule about whether networks can be successfully drawn or not. Encourage them to devise their own versions of the Towers of Hanoi puzzle and other logic games in which items have to be moved to new positions.

KEY VOCABULARY

Algebra, sign, symbol, stands for, represents, digit, one-, two- and three-digit numbers, commutative law, associative law, inverse operation, number statement, number sentence, 3D, three dimensional, cube, cuboid, triangular prism, tetrahedron, squared-based pyramid, vertices, edges, faces, network, junction, route, odd, even, method, strategy, what could we try next, how did it work out.

NATIONAL NUMERACY STRATEGY LINKS

Year 4
Oral and mental starter

- Consolidate understanding of relationship between + and –.
- Understand the principles (not the names) of the commutative and associative laws as they apply, or not, to addition and subtraction.
- Extend understanding of the operations of x and ÷ and their relationship to each other and also + and –.
- Use the relationship between multiplication and division.
- Check with the inverse operation.
- Check the sum of several numbers by adding in reverse order. Check with an equivalent calculation.

Main teaching activity

- Choose and use appropriate number operations and appropriate ways of calculating.
- Solve mathematical problems or puzzles.
- Make and investigate a general statement about familiar shapes by finding examples that satisfy it.
- Describe and visualise 3D shapes.

Year 6
Oral and mental starter

As Year 4 plus:

- Develop further the relationship between addition and subtraction.
- Understand the effect of the relationship between the four operations and the principles (not the names) of the arithmetic laws as they apply to multiplication.

Main teaching activity

As Year 4 plus:

- Explain methods and reasoning orally and in writing.
- Explain a generalised relationship (formula) in words.

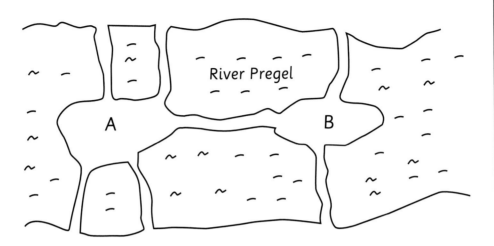

On warm summer evenings the people of Königsberg like to stroll around their riverside town. Part of the town is made up of two islands in the middle of the River Pregel. Island A is joined to the rest of the town by four bridges; Island B is joined by two bridges and the two islands are also linked by a bridge.

Is it possible to plan a route around the town starting at one place and finishing at the same location which allows all seven bridges to be crossed once only?

Show the starting/finishing place and mark the route walked, putting arrows on the path to show which way you went.

There are two similar problems below. Using the same rules, is it possible to find routes for these?

- To play this game you will need a playing board like this:

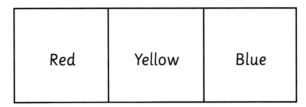

| Red | Yellow | Blue |

- Also make three card discs about $2\frac{1}{2}$ cm, 2 cm and $1\frac{1}{2}$ cm in radius.

- Stack the discs in order of size on the red section. The smallest disc must be on top.

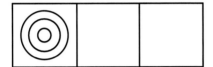 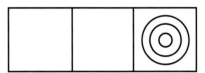

- The purpose of the game is to move all three discs to the blue section, keeping them in the same size order.

You MUST follow these rules:
- large discs cannot be placed on smaller ones;
- you can only move one disc at a time;
- you can only move the top disc in any pile;
- you can place any disc in any of the sections;
- you cannot place discs side by side in the same section, only on top of each other.

- How many moves did it take to get the discs from red to blue?
- What is the least number of moves needed to get the discs from the red to the blue square?
- Try the game again, this time moving discs from the red to the yellow square.

Born at Leipzig in Germany in 1646, he was largely self-taught as a youngster, doing much of his early learning in the library of his father, who taught at the city's university. By the age of eight he was able to speak Latin and four years later had also mastered Greek. Leibniz went on to study at Leipzig University himself and also at Jena and Altdorf before qualifying as a lawyer. In 1667, he joined the staff of the ruler of Mainz, where he spent most of his working time trying to improve laws and also drafting a scheme for the unity of churches in the area. As a hobby he studied philosophy, science and mathematics and became particularly interested in the writings of René Descartes and Blaise Pascal from France and the Englishman Isaac Newton.

Leibniz moved to Paris in 1672 as a political adviser and this gave him the opportunity to travel to other countries. Among the places he visited were Holland and England, and while in London he had several meetings with Newton. The two men had numerous ideas to share and found that independently they had been working on many of the same problems in both maths and science.

By 1676 he had returned to Germany and for the last 40 years of his life worked as an adviser and librarian, first for the Duke of Brunswick and later for George, the Elector of Hanover, who in 1714 became King George I of Great Britain. Unlike many other famous mathematicians, Leibniz was never a rich man and had no wealthy sponsors. He always needed a paid job and as a result was restricted to working on his other interests during his spare time. In 1700 he persuaded King Frederick of Prussia to establish the Prussian Academy of Sciences in Berlin; the King did Leibniz the honour of making him its first President. Always a very religious man, Leibniz believed that God was the source of all things and that he lived in the best of all possible worlds because God had created it.

Throughout his life, Leibniz was a great believer in trying to make education as practical as possible. He himself worked on trying to improve a wide range of equipment, including presses, lamps, submarines, clocks and windmills. But, as one would expect of a philosopher, he also wrote that all knowledge and experience originated in thinking. He stressed that the aim of education was the mastery of thinking and judgement and not just the gathering of facts.

The main interest that Leibniz shared with Newton was their work on an extension of algebra that is known as calculus. This branch of mathematics investigates and tries to establish rules about the way in which things change, such as the speed at which objects travel a certain distance in a given time. Leibniz's system was first published in 1684, Newton's followed three years later. Calculus remains important in all areas of science and technology, especially to engineers, who use it to look at the strength of structures and the performance of machines.

Leibniz's other achievements include the development of the binary, or base 2, system and the invention of a simple calculating machine. The binary system is widely used now in electronics and computing. In this method of counting all numbers are shown using only the digits 0 and 1. To Leibniz, 1 represented God while 0 was the void, or nothingness. The first working model of his calculating machine was completed in 1673. It could not only add and subtract but also multiply, divide and work out square roots.

PLACE VALUE

Before starting to look at binary numbers ensure that the children are secure in their understanding of the base 10 or denary counting system which they use for most of their calculations. Provide them with a range of practical activities that will give them the ability to write larger and larger numbers in both figures and words.

Activities

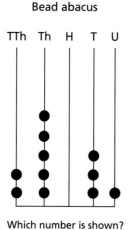

Bead abacus

TTh Th H T U

Which number is shown?

● **Figure 10.1**

Bead abacus

HTh TTh Th H T U

Show the number 653, 274 on the abacus

● **Figure 10.2**

Bead abacus drawings is one method that can be used. Children can either read off the number that is shown (Figure 10.1) or mark on the correct number of beads for the given amount (Figure 10.2). Also give plenty of practice with the type of washing line and peg activity described in previous chapters when looking at both the use of 0 and decimal numbers.

Use four-, five- or six-digit cards now and vary the scope of the questions as much as possible. For example, if the cards 4, 2, 6, 7, 5 were made available, questions could include:

- What is the largest number that can be made?
- What is the smallest number that can be made?
- Which number would be closest to 50,000?
- Which number would be closest to 100,000?
- What is the largest even number that can be made?
- What is the smallest odd number that can be made?
- What numbers can be made between 2,000 and 4,000?
- Take all the numbers that can be made starting with the 6 and place them in order of size beginning with the smallest.

Key signs < and >

Also take this opportunity to revise the key signs < and > and the type of language work they help to generate. Stress that the open part of the sign always points towards the larger number and that statements should always be read from the left-hand side, for example, 4,321 > 4,213 is read as four thousand three hundred and twenty one is larger than four thousand two hundred and thirteen. On the other hand, 1,528 < 2,581 is read as one thousand five hundred and twenty eight is smaller than two thousand five hundred and eighty one.

Rounding numbers

This is also an ideal time to sharpen up on rounding off numbers to the nearest 10, 100 or 1,000. Explain that numbers up to the halfway point (5, 50 and 500) are rounded down, while numbers at halfway or more are rounded up. Use numbers to check on all three rules at the same time; for example: What is 4,356 to the nearest ten, hundred and thousand? (4,360, 4,400 and 4,000.)

Working with base 2

As Leibniz proposed, the binary or base 2 system uses only the digits 1 and 0. These are often also seen in terms of 1 for on and 0 for off, or 1 for open and 0 for closed. The big disadvantage in using this system is that even small numbers have to be represented with a large number of digits. The advantage, in computer terms, is that because only two digits are used, the recall of numbers is extremely rapid. The large number of digits is also not a problem because of the computer's vast memory. Whereas in the denary system column headings get ten times bigger as they move from right to the left, so with binary numbers each new heading is made by multiplying by 2. So, for numbers up to 64, the headings would be 64, 32, 16, 8, 4, 2 and 1. How the numbers as far as 15 are made up in the binary system is shown in Figure 10.3.

	32	16	8	4	2	1
1						1
2					1	0
3					1	1
4				1	0	0
5				1	0	1
6				1	1	0
7				1	1	1
8			1	0	0	0
9			1	0	0	1
10			1	0	1	0
11			1	0	1	1
12			1	1	0	0
13			1	1	0	1
14			1	1	1	0
15			1	1	1	1

• **Figure 10.3:** Binary numbers to 15

Binary games

One of the best ways to introduce children to binary numbers is through playing practical games. Two of these are described now. The first one is called Stand Up, and the second, Think of a Number.

In Stand Up, sit five children across the room in a row (Figure 10.4). Each child holds in front of him or her a card showing, from left to right, 16, 8, 4, 2 and 1. Choose another child to act as a caller. When the caller says '1', the child holding that card stands up. On the call of '2', the child with the 2 card stands up and the holder of the 1 card sits down. When 3 is called, both these children will stand to make 11 (one 2 and one 1), which is the binary number for 3; '4' will lead to the holder of the 4 card standing, with the others sitting down. This number is being shown as 100 representing one 4, no 2s and no 1s. 5 is shown in Figure 10.4, and the process should then be continued until 16 is reached. After a while it should become obvious that a cardholder only moves, to stand or sit, when the cardholder on his or her immediate left sits down. It should also be noted that the person holding the 1 card does the largest share of the work. Ask the children to explain why this is. A more difficult task is to ask the human binary counting machine to show base 10 numbers at random, for example, 19 or 25. They then have to decide among themselves who should be sitting and who should be standing.

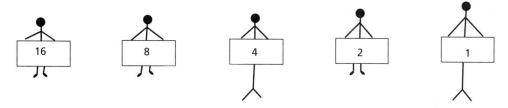

Child 'Four' and Child 'One' standing to show 5 in the binary system. The rest are sitting

● **Figure 10.4:** The Stand Up game

To play the game Think of a Number, the set of six of six cards shown on the photocopiable sheet at the end of the chapter should be mounted on thin card and cut out. The numbers have been generated by turning all the numbers between 1 and 63 into their base 2 equivalents using the method given in Figure 10.3. The card starting with 1 shows all the binary numbers where a 1 has to be included; the card commencing with 2, all the numbers which use 2; the 4 card, 4; and so on. The game should be played in pairs. One child asks another to think of any number between 1 and 63. They should write it down secretly but not say it aloud. The child who has thought of the number is then shown each of the six cards in turn. They should on no account say the number they are thinking of, but should say yes or no if the number appears on the cards that they are shown. The cardholder should put the 'yes' cards into one pile and the 'no' cards into another. The cardholder finds the missing number by counting up the first number to feature on each of the cards in the 'yes' pile. For example, if a child chose 25, he or she should say yes to the card beginning with 1, no to the card beginning with 2, no to the card starting with 4, yes to the cards commencing with 8 and 16 and no to the card beginning with 32. Adding together the first number on each of the 'yes' cards, namely 1, 8 and 16, would yield the missing number 25. This should work every time.

Ancient number systems

Converting our current base 10 numbers into number systems that have been used in the past can extend this work on the binary system. Roman numerals, for example, are still found in many places and children can become fascinated with the way in which ancient civilisations such as the Babylonians, the Egyptians and the Mayans used to do their counting. Take the opportunity also to look at codes where letters are changed into numbers to send simple messages. Several examples are given in Figure 10.5.

<u>1</u>

A	B	C	D	E	F	G	H	I	J	K	L	M	N	O	P	Q
1	2	3	4	5	6	7	8	9	10	11	12	13	14	15	16	17

R	S	T	U	V	W	X	Y	Z
18	19	20	21	22	23	24	25	26

<u>2</u>

A	B	C	D	E	F	G	H	I	J	K	L	M	N	O	P	Q
3	6	9	12	15	18	21	24	27	30	33	36	39	42	45	48	51

R	S	T	U	V	W	X	Y	Z
54	57	60	63	66	69	72	75	78

<u>3</u>

A	B	C	D	E	F	G	H	I	J	K	L	M	N	O	P	Q
52	50	48	46	44	42	40	38	36	34	32	30	28	26	24	22	20

R	S	T	U	V	W	X	Y	Z
18	16	14	12	10	8	6	4	2

• **Figure 10.5:** Examples of simple number codes

Using the calculator

There are good reasons for not over-using the calculator with Key Stage 2 children: the ability to work out answers mentally and by using traditional pencil and paper methods will always be important. Yet for some activities the calculator is an invaluable tool as its use allows children to get straight to the heart of the mathe-matical process. Among these activities are problems that involve dealing with very big numbers and investigations where numerous calculations need to be done rapidly. Some examples of this first group are given on the photocopiable sheet *Taking your time*, and working with magic squares is a good way of practising the second. Magic squares – first devised by the Chinese thousands of years ago – have lines, horizontally, vertically and diagonally, that add up to the same total. A simple example of a magic square is shown in Figure 10.6, and Figure 10.7 gives others which children can investigate with their calculators, using either two-digit or minus numbers.

5	10	3
4	6	8
9	2	7

Magic square total = 18   ● **Figure 10.6**

Solve these magic squares:

10	20	
	12	
		14

10	35	
	25	
		40

−2	3	2
	1	
		4

● **Figure 10.7**

SUPPORT

Give the children plenty of place value work using abacus drawings and washing line tasks before moving on. Make sure their understanding of place value involving two- and three-digit numbers is secure before moving to larger numbers. Structured apparatus such as multibase and charts showing hundreds, tens and units columns may have to be used to help understanding. Support will need to be given when converting numbers into base 2. Restrict to numbers up to 20 initially. Provide plenty of demonstrations of the binary game called Stand Up and issue written instructions for playing Think of a Number, if necessary. An introduction to the position of the keys on the calculator and their functions will be necessary for children who are not familiar with them.

EXTENSION

Extend place value tasks to reach a million for those who are capable. Spend time on writing large numbers in both figures and words. Encourage children to use quick ways of multiplying and dividing whole numbers by ten and one hundred and to be able to round off easily in order to work out approximate answers quickly. Children may be able to extend the Stand Up game by adding a 32 card and add a seventh card to Think of a Number so that it can accommodate numbers up to 127. They should be able to research and then explore alternative number systems in more detail and devise their own number/letter codes for sending secret messages.

KEY VOCABULARY

Place value, notation, units, ones, tens, hundreds, thousands, ten thousands, hundred thousands, millions, round up to, round down to, approximate, greater than, more than, larger than, bigger than, less than, fewer than, smaller than, denary system, base 10, binary system, base 2, calculator, display, key, enter, clear, sign, change, memory, operation key, magic square.

RESOURCES

Blank sheets of abacus drawings, washing line, pegs, digit cards, structured base 10 apparatus, place value column sheets, large binary number cards, thin card, scissors, glue, examples of alternative number systems, for example, Roman numerals, calculators, magic squares, squared paper, photocopiable pages 116 and 117.

NATIONAL NUMERACY STRATEGY LINKS

Year 4
Oral and mental starter

- Find a small difference by counting up.
- Count on or back in repeated steps of 1, 10 and 100.
- Partition into tens and units, adding the tens first.
- Use known number facts and place value to add or subtract mentally, including any pair of two-digit numbers.
- Use known number facts and place value to multiply and divide integers, including by 10 and then by 100.

Main teaching activity

- Read and write whole numbers to at least 10,000 in figures and words and know what each digit represents.
- Add/subtract 1,10,100 or 1000 to/from any integer and count on or back in tens, hundreds or thousands from any whole number up to 10,000.
- Read and write the vocabulary of comparing and ordering.
- Use symbols correctly, including less than (<), greater than (>) and equals (=).
- Round any positive integer less than 1000 to the nearest 10 or 100.
- Solve mathematical problems or puzzles, recognise and explain patterns and relationships, generalise and predict.

Year 6
Oral and mental starter

As Year 4 plus:

- Find differences by counting up through next multiple of 10, 100 or 1000.
- Partition into H, T and U adding the most significant digit first.
- Use known number facts and place value to multiply and divide mentally.

Main teaching activity

As Year 4 plus:

- Read and write whole numbers in figures and words and know what each digit represents.
- Multiply and divide any positive integer up to 10,000 by 10 or 100 and understand the effect.
- Round any integer up to 10,000 to the nearest 10, 100 or 1000.
- Develop calculator skills and use a calculator effectively.
- Choose and use appropriate number operations to solve problems and appropriate ways of calculating.

You will need these cards to play the game called Think of a Number.

Mount the sheet on thin card to make it stronger before cutting the cards out.

These cards will allow your friends to choose any number up to 63.

1	3	5	7	9	11	13	15
17	19	21	23	25	27	29	31
33	35	37	39	41	43	45	47
49	51	53	55	57	59	61	63

2	3	6	7	10	11	14	15
18	19	22	23	26	27	30	31
34	35	38	39	42	43	46	47
50	51	54	55	58	59	62	63

4	5	6	7	12	13	14	15
20	21	22	23	28	29	30	31
36	37	38	39	44	45	46	47
52	53	54	55	60	61	62	63

8	9	10	11	12	13	14	15
24	25	26	27	28	29	30	31
40	41	42	43	44	45	46	47
56	57	58	59	60	61	62	63

16	17	18	19	20	21	22	23
24	25	26	27	28	29	30	31
48	49	50	51	52	53	54	55
56	57	58	59	60	61	62	63

32	33	34	35	36	37	38	39
40	41	42	43	44	45	46	47
48	49	50	51	52	53	54	55
56	57	58	59	60	61	62	63

If you are going to play the game with a large group of children you may need to make a larger set of the game cards so that they can see them from a distance.

Fact box

There are 365 days in a year, but every fourth year there is a leap year which has 366 days.

1 If today is your eleventh birthday, how many days have you lived?

2 Work out your real age in days.

3 Work out the ages in days of two of your friends.

4 How many days have there been since the Coronation of Queen Elizabeth II on 2 June 1953?

5 How many years are there in 250,000 days? Assume that there are 365.25 days in each year.

6 How many hours do you work at school in a week, a term, a school year?

7 How many days have you been at school altogether?

8 If you could change the system of clocks and the calendar, what improvements would you make?

• For each of the questions 1–7 show how you used the calculator by writing down what you did and your working out.

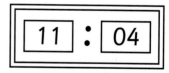

Answers and Solutions

CHAPTER 1: ERATOSTHENES

Figure 1.3:

From start to finish 25, 15, 10, 5, 30, 20, 40, 35, 50, 45.

Photocopiable Sheet 1:

(a) From 6 to 66 using multiples of 6: 6, 216, 690, 474, 492, 294, 108, 96, 408, 384, 774, 666, 432, 612, 168, 372, 144 and 66.

(b) From 7 to 77: 7, 35, 28, 392, 455, 385, 693, 336, 777, 217, 28, 63, 287 and 77.

Photocopiable Sheet 2: The 25 prime numbers, not including 1, are 2, 3, 5, 7, 11, 13, 17, 19, 23, 29, 31, 37, 41, 43, 47, 53, 59, 61, 67, 71, 73, 79, 83, 89 and 97.

CHAPTER 2: NAPIER

Photocopiable Sheet 4: Answers to decimal flowers:

1) 1.5 + 1.9 = 3.4 and 4.0 – 0.6 = 3.4
2) 4.7 + 7.8 = 12.5 and 14.2 – 1.7 = 12.5
3) 9.4 + 5.8 = 15.2 and 17.3 – 2.1 = 15.2
4) 6.67 + 3.15 = 9.82 and 20.47 – 10.65 = 9.82

CHAPTER 3: PASCAL

Figure 3.2:

```
        22                          28
     13    9                    15       13
   7   6   3                  8    7       6
 3   4   2   1              5    3     4       2
```

Figure 3.7:

```
          3
       8      7
     4          6
  2     5  9       1
```

Figure 3.8:

```
1       3
6   4   2
5       7
```

Figure 3.10:

```
        5
30          35
6       42   7
```

CHAPTER 4: FIBONACCI

Photocopiable Sheet 8: Number chains:

3	1	4	5	9
9	11	20	31	51
5	6	11	17	28
8	12	20	32	52
15	10	25	35	60
1	3½	4½	8	12½

CHAPTER 5: DESCARTES

Photocopiable Sheet 9:

Shapes are 1) triangle, 2) square, 3) rectangle, 4) pentagon.

CHAPTER 6: ARCHIMEDES

Figure 6.7:

Actual numbers of parts of circle: 2   4   8   16   31

CHAPTER 7: EUCLID

Figure 7.2: Missing numbers on the dice:

```
        4          5 4              4
1    5  6  2          6 2       1  5
        3              3 1         3  6
                                      2
```

Figure 8.2: Continuation of triad patterns:

Side A	Side B	Side C
11	60	61
13	84	85
15	112	113
17	144	145
19	180	181

Figure 8.11

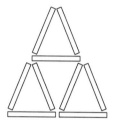

Figure 8.12

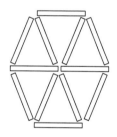

Figure 8.13:

(a) Three coins need to be moved: they are the three corner ones.
(b) Coins should be placed like this to make 5 pence on each side:

```
            2p
      1p          1p
  2p        1p        2p
```

Figure 8.14:

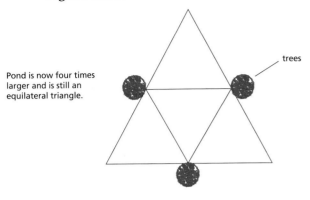

Pond is now four times larger and is still an equilateral triangle.

trees

Photocopiable Sheet 16:

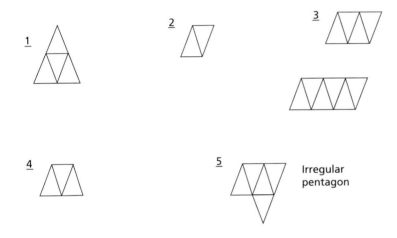

1

2

3

4

5   Irregular pentagon

CHAPTER 9: EULER

Figure 9.1:

$$
\begin{array}{r}
543 \\
+\ \ 21 \\
\hline
564
\end{array}
$$

Figure 9.2:

$$
\begin{array}{r}
123 \\
-\ 54 \\
\hline
69
\end{array}
$$

Figure 9.3:   L = 4 and M = 5; A = 2, T = 3 and P = 9.

CHAPTER 10: LEIBNIZ

Figure 10.7:

10	20	6		10	35	30		-2	+3	+2
8	12	16		45	25	5		+5	+1	-3
18	4	14		20	15	40		0	-1	+4

Total is 36   Total is 75   Total is +3

Photocpiable Sheet 20:

4) It was 17,013 days up until the end of 1999.

5) It is 684 years to the nearest year.

Index

Alexandria 3, 4, 62, 72
Algebra 96–97
Ancient number systems 112
Angles in triangles and quadrilaterals 86
Area of a circle 65–66,
Area of a triangle 87–88
Archimedes 61–62
Archimedes Principle 63, 69
Associative law (addition and multiplication) 97
Aswan 4

Big numbers 117
Binary numbers 110 –111, 116

Calculators 112–113
Cartesian co-ordinates 50–51, 58
Circle investigations 66–67
Commutative law (addition and multiplication) 97

Data handling and graphs 52–53
Decimal numbers 20–21, 25
Descartes, René 27, 49–50, 108
Digital roots 5

Earth's circumference 4
Egypt 3, 4
Eratosthenes 3–5, 62
Euclid 27, 40, 50, 62, 71–72
Euler, Leonhard 95–96
Euler's rule for 3D shapes 99

Factors 5, 7–9
Fibonacci, Leonardo 28, 39–40
Fibonacci sequence of numbers 40–43, 47

Gelosia method of multiplying 17–18
Grids 51–52, 58

Hanoi, The Towers of 105

Index numbers 50, 54–55
Inverse operations 98

Konigsberg, The Bridges of 104

Leibniz, Gottfried 107–108

Magic squares 113

Metrilogs 65
Mobius band 101
Multiples 5
Multiplication methods 18–19

Napier, John 15–16
Napier's bones for calculations 16–17, 24
Networks 99–100
Newton, Isaac 108
Number mazes 5, 12
Number chains 48

Parallel lines 77–78
Pascal, Blaise 27–28, 108
Pascal's triangle 28, 36
Pi 64–66, 70
Pisa 39–40
Place value 109
Platonic polyhedra 74–76
Positive and negative numbers 54, 59
Prime numbers 5, 7–9, 13
Probability and chance 32–33
Pyramid numbers 29
Pythagoras 40, 62, 83–84
Pythagoras' Theorem 84–85, 92

Reflective symmetry 10
Rounding off numbers 110

Slide rulers 19
Spirals 43
Square numbers 44–45

Tessellation 88, 93
Time 117
3D shapes 64, 73–76, 80–81, 99
Times tables 5–6
Triangular numbers 29–30
Triangles in construction 76–77
Triangles-balanced numbers 30–32
Triangle families 87
Triangle games 89
2D shapes 37, 76–78, 89

Venn diagrams 6
Volume 63–64

Zero 40, 43–44